Mischievous Rascal

Mischievous Rascal

Taylor Samuel Lyen

iUniverse, Inc.
New York Lincoln Shanghai

Mischievous Rascal

iUniverse, Inc.

For information address:
iUniverse, Inc.
2021 Pine Lake Road, Suite 100
Lincoln, NE 68512
www.iuniverse.com

ISBN: 0-595-31633-6 (pbk)
ISBN: 0-595-66348-6 (cloth)

Printed in the United States of America

Marie, Michael, Ben, Connie, Diane,
Kim, Jason, and Megan

Contents

Acknowledgements

I am indebted to the family, friends, colleagues, and acquaintances, who have, over the years, graciously shared their thoughts and experiences with me. I deeply value your insights and hope you realize how truly indispensable you were to my writing this story.

Adeyinka Fashokun, Ed.D

A. J. Petersdorpf, M.A.

Annie Herda, Ed.D., Ph.D

Blanche and Sam

Bob Hagler, M.A.

Bob Vernagallo, M.A. M.B.A.

Brian A. Girard, Ph.D

Bruce Gidlund, M.S.

Carol Haberberger, M.A

Clare LePell

Connie Castellanos, M.A

Dalene Trinchero-Johnson

Dan & Gail & Megan

Dan-Dan The Sunshine Man

Darlene Philippe

Darlene Santos, M.A

Diane Aranda, M.P.A.

Dixie Hall

Elaine McEntee

Kelly Densmore

LaRue Neil

Len Strodbeck, M.A.

Lieutenant Richard Lucia

Linda Falt

Linda McKinley

Liz Blasquez, Ed.D.

Lori Miller, M.A.

Luella Bois

Lyle Mickin

Maggie Cathey, M.A.

Marvin Smith, Ed.D.

Murphy Taylor, M.A

Nancy McMillan, Ph.D.

Nicanor & Chayo

Nina

Paul A. Opler, Ph.D.

Peter E. Livanos, Jr. J.D.

Peter Hansen, M.A.

Elisbeth "Libby" Wrede

Father Patrick Duffy, J.D., Ph.D.

Fran Ebert, Ed.D.

Gary Mathiason, J.D.

Glenna Kenitzer

Honorable Judge Larry Goodman

Jack McKay, M.S.

Jamie Boasso

Jean Pfeiffer

Jenny Lin Foundation

Jessica & Richard Barrett, D.V.M

Jim Fitzpatrick, M.A.

Jim Murphy

Jo & Ed Loss

Joe Farias, M.A.

John Robinson, Ph.D.

Judy & Jerry Guerino, J.D.

Project Eden/Horizon Services

Rev. Charles Johnstone, Ph.D

Rev. JoAnne Bennett, MDIV

Richard Kuensting

Robert Alioto, Ph.D.

Robin Kurotori

Shirley Baptiste, Ed.D.

Susan Belone

Susan & Darrell Ubick, M.A.

The Shermanator

Tim Ghazaleh

Trish Feucht

Wardess Taylor

Wendy & Don Ruffner

Wes Jones

William C. Schriner, Ph.D.

Wixon Family

To the children and parents whom I have had the honor
to serve during forty years in public education,
my eternal gratitude.

To Fran Aahl & Jan Keller of ABC Nursery (Castro Valley, CA),
to Jean Lucido, M.S., M.F.T. & Johnny Burks, M.A., M.S.
of Project Re-Connect (Oakland, CA) my gratitude
for allowing me to learn from the excellent
work you do with children and youth.

Text Notes

Superscripted small case letters found throughout the story refer to pictures, which are located in the Family Photo Album section of the Appendix. Superscripted numbers found throughout the story refer to citations and comments, which are located in the Endnotes section of the Appendix. All other source references are embedded in the text of the story.

Author's Note

Mischievous Rascal is the story of a mother's unflagging zeal to correctly raise her mischievous rascal of a son and of that rascal's search, some sixty plus years later, to understand his mother's fury and his father's ghostly presence. As with the births, lives, and deaths of stars within constellations, galaxies, and the universe, so humans are born, live out their lives, and die within families, social institutions, and societies. After passing on, stars leave behind only faint traces of their existences. Humans do this as well. So, it is up to us to piece together those traces to reveal our stories for all to see and from which all may learn.

Since the beginning of humankind, stargazers have looked to the heavens, observed the paths of heavenly bodies, and gave meaning and purpose to what they saw. In like fashion, Blanche Greenstone watched her newborn son, a persistent star, grow and develop from 1939 onward. Meticulously recording her observations and candidly sharing her opinions about her only child, Blanche adorned the pages of *Our Baby Book* with her hopes, dreams, aspirations, concerns, and fears about her only child Thomas. From the beginning to the end of *Our Baby Book,* Blanche Greenstone's unvarnished writings unveil as much about herself as she unveils about the early life and times of her son. Blanche tells how she crossed into motherhood on the highest pinnacles of human joy. Then, she exposes her innermost feelings, as she traveled deeper into the unknown and forbidding forests of parenting and walked helplessly on the dark canyon floors of frustration and despair.

Blanche Greenstone's writing[gg] gives us only an indirect glimpse of Sam Greenstone, Thomas's father, an enigmatic star from an English/Scottish family constellation. As we shall find out from Thomas's recollections, Sam's presence held considerable sway throughout Thomas's life, although his fatherly influence had been dwarfed by the intensity and dominance of the brightest and most volatile star in Thomas's life, his mother Blanche. Content with being lost in the brilliance of his wife's corona and mantled in constant and profound pain, Sam ambled quietly through life with a pronounced limp caused by degenerative hip condition. He never complained, instead he stoically accepted his fate with the aide of a cocktail or two and Percodan.

To more fully appreciate our *Mischievous Rascal*, we need to take a multi-generational look at the Freitas and Greenstone families. Consequently, our story is told within several settings. Part I of our story touches on the religious, social, and historical/political contexts within which Thomas's grandparents and parents were born and the influences theses times had on their lives. Part II focuses on the relationships and interactions within Thomas's immediate family, as seen through Blanche's eyes and Thomas's recollections. Part III examines the relationships and interactions within the Greenstone family and sets the know facts against the findings of child psychology and the research on child growth and development. In addition, the good, the bad, and the ugly behaviors of Blanche and Sam, as parents, and of individuals working within social institutions, (e.g., teachers, priests, ministers, and youth directors) are analyzed and discussed in relationship to their affects on Thomas, in particular, and their affects on children, in general. Part IV mulls over the role that chance or God played in Thomas's life, plays in the lives of Thomas's children, (Kim and Michael), plays in the life of Thomas's grandchild (Megan Adams), and plays in our lives. Lastly, Part V delves into questions about the choices parents and grandparents can make to influence their progeny and their progeny's families in positive ways.

All in all, our story cuts and studies but a minuscule section of the human continuum, a brief flicker of time from 1880 through 2004 that takes place in the evolution of one family. As readers, we will subject the exhumed bits and pieces of the Greenstone family's history to what medical examiners describe as a preliminary assessment at the scene of the "crime." As we observe carefully the unfolding of the Greenstone family history and the unfolding of other family histories, including our own histories, we open windows to better view the world outside and to better understand our inner beings. Moreover, by sharing our personal or family stories, we gain a more complete picture of our life's purpose within the course of human affairs. Finding a positive path for our lives and knowing where human progress should be taking us gives us wonderful insights and holds the promise that we can make the world a little better place to live in, and that ain't bad.

Finally, as a condition of writing the *Mischievous Rascal*, this author agreed to be suitably vague, respecting the true identity of Dr. Thomas Greenstone. However, the events recorded in *Our Baby Book*, Greenstone's adult recollections of his childhood and youth, and the analytical review of Blanche, Sam, and Thomas's life and times are true and factual, as are the accounts of Megan, Marie and Thomas's granddaughter, and all of the other individuals drawn into our story.

TSL
8/16/04

Foreword

"You're going to be grandparents. And, we want Michael to be the godfather," announced our daughter Kim. This news of our first grandchild from our first child immediately and that Kim's brother Michael was to be the Godfather sent my mind racing back sixty years to my own godparents and the part they played in my life. Not only had my parents known my godparents years before they married, they had lived, worked, and raised their children in the same building—a mortuary in Oakland, California.

My mother penned her earliest observations and thoughts about me in a baby book along with a photographic chronology of my activities. As I was cleaning my attic one spring day, I saw a box that had been placed behind the chimney. After I retrieved the box, I found several photo albums and *Our Baby Book*. I read the baby book from cover to cover. When finished with the book, I began on the first of five photo albums, which memorialized my life, the lives of my godparents, the lives of my parents, and the lives of their parents. I realized that in my hands were all the stars of my past family constellations reaching back in time. Thoughts, emotions, sensations, places, friends, teachers, relationships, and other recollections large and small welled up from preconscious rivers as fresh as the day they were made. Then came the questions and more questions. I was fascinated and astonished by my need to now make a complete picture, not just of my early experiences, but the experiences and lives of those earlier generations.

And so, six months before Megan joined us by becoming the latest member of the newest triadic family constellation, the Adams Family, I began my journey backward into my family history.

Respectfully,

Dr. Thomas Zechariah Greenstone
1/16/03

PART I

STARS, LIKE HUMANS, ARE BORN IN FAMILY CONSTELLATIONS

*"In ancient times humans imagined they could see figures in
the night when lines were drawn connecting adjacent stars."
(Audubon Society Field Guide to the Night Sky (2000), p. 77)*

*"Let now the astrologers, the stargazers, the monthly prognosticators
stand up, and save thee from these things that shall come upon thee."
(Isaiah 47.13 King James Version of the Holy Bible)*

Mischievous Rascal is a story, which details the interpersonal relationships and interactions within the Greenstone family: Sam Greenstone[i], Blanche (Freitas)[j] Greenstone, and their only son Thomas. Our story follows the affects of family dynamics through Thomas's childhood, fatherhood, and grand fatherhood. To find the amber in which the early pieces of the Greenstone family are embedded, we need to step back several generations and reconstruct the religious, social, and political times within which Blanche and Sam's parents lived and, which in turn, influenced the lives of Blanche and Sam before they met, fell in love, and decided to raise a family.

You will notice that our historical search focuses on President Theodore Roosevelt. Whether we know it or not, the persona and behaviors of the men and women in the White House, to a greater or lesser degree, shape and reinforce family attitudes, the content of topics discussed around the house, and help weave the linguistic fabric of our families. A recent 2004 example, President

George W. Bush and First Lady Laura Bush illustrate this point. In the Bush administration, there are clear right and clear wrong answers to religious and political issues—few, if any, shades of gray. Take a moment to consider how these issues and attitudes from the President and the First Lady play out in or affect your family—around the dinner table, casual conversations, family values, et cetera? Though your answers may range from no to great influence on your family, families, nonetheless, by the nature of the government in which they are embedded, are forced to deal with the question and thereby affect or energize family attitudes, discussions, and values. In short, whether we like it or not, or whether we admit it or not, events in the White House are intertwined with events in our family. Turning to the first historically influential President and First Lady in Thomas's parents and grandparents' times, Theodore "Teddy" Roosevelt and Edith Roosevelt, did the events in the White House affect the Freitas and Greenstone families? This question leads us to place an emphasis on the life and times of Teddy Roosevelt (Edith Roosevelt was not a politically active First Lady. Recall that not too long ago most First Ladies did not share photo opts with their President-husbands, let share the political limelight.) in relation to how Teddy's behaviors and policies affected the Greenstone and Freitas families, in general, and Sam Greenstone, Thomas's father in particular.

We begin by familiarizing ourselves with the lives of Blanche and Sam's parents: Phillip Greenstone and Margaret Hurst (Sam's parents) and Joe Freitas and Mary Valladao (Blanche's parents)—all of whom affected Thomas's life by their interactions with Thomas, the hearing of family lore, and through the actions Sam and Blanche.[k]

Stars of Generations Passed

In 1886, Margaret E. Hurst (Sam's mother) was born in Pinesville, Kentucky.[a] In that same year Phillip Mathew Greenstone (Sam's father) was a six-years-old boy, living and playing in the bluegrass hills of Kirkwood, Kentucky.[a] From what Thomas has gathered from his relatives, currently living in and around Lexington Kentucky, the Greenstone family was respected and financially well off. One family photo, which was taken in 1915, shows the family standing on the steps of a splendid Victorian house, flanked by a variety of servants. The major accumulators of wealth in the Greenstone family were medical doctors, lawyers, and morticians. However, Phillip Greenstone appears to have come from the poor-side of the Greenstone family and, in 1907 moved with his wife Margaret and three-year-old daughter from Kentucky to Long Beach, California.[e, f] Thomas has no recollection of his Grandpa Phillip, as Phillip died in April 1942 at Saint Mary's

Hospital, when Thomas was two and one-half years old. Over the years, Thomas has been told several stories about how Grandpa Phillip died—appendicitis is the frontrunner. The fact is that Phillip, at sixty-two years of age, never had a chance to bond with his grandson and became a Never star in Thomas's memory.

Contrary to the picture of Margaret taken in 1910, Thomas remembers his Grandma Margaret, as a very old, craggy, stooped-shouldered, chain-smoking Broken star, which always wore a crest-fallen, rumpled long black cloth coat. No one ever told Thomas that Grandma Margaret suffered the ravages of alcoholism, which accounted for her emaciated appearance in 1945, a picture fixed in her grandson's memory. After Phillip died, Margaret continued to live in Long Beach with Kenny, Sam's younger brother, until she passed away in 1948. Word of Grandma Margaret's death never came to Thomas's ears through family members.

Mary Constance Valladao (Blanche's mother) was born on the Island of Flores in the Azores on January 27, 1888.[b] At that time, Joseph Freitas, Jr. (Blanche's father) was a five-year-old lad playing in the golden hills of Alamo, California.[b] Family records and photos show that Joe's family were orchard farmers, growing cherries, apricots, and walnuts, and that Mary's family were ranchers and dairy farmers in the old country, Portugal. Thomas vividly remembers his Grandma Freitas and Grandpa Joe, as he spent several summers with them. Sam and Blanche also brought Thomas with them to Martinez every single weekend and on holidays to visit his grandparents and play with his cousins. Later, Thomas, his wife Marie, and their two children, Kim and Michael, continued to visit Grandma Freitas, until her death in 1973. To this day, Kim and Michael clearly remember their Great Grandmother Freitas in Martinez.

Mary Freitas left quite an impression on her grandson Thomas. Of all the people who cared for him, Grandma Freitas in Martinez remains at the top of his list. The small, gentle, sensible woman with waves of slivery hair and silvery curls hugging her face brought feelings of comfort, belonging, and assurance to Thomas. Grandma Freitas loved to bake and cook for her family and seemed to whip up specialties for Thomas every time he went to Martinez. A devout Catholic, Grandma's religion was Portuguese sweet bread, three-layer vanilla frosted white cakes, and a glass of cold milk. Grandma commanded the absolute respect of all family members not by demanding, but by loving and serving. She was no push over, however. There was no cussing or rough play in or outside of the house, when Grandma Freitas was in sight—Grandma ruled the roost. Her limited English vocabulary got the message across in no uncertain terms. "Go to grass!" was one of the phrases she spoke; and with that, the grandchildren who were getting a little out of hand would immediately settle down. Grandma Freitas brought constancy into Thomas's life. She was his Constant star, a star he thinks about daily.

Grandpa Joe, on the other hand, was an uncomplicated, volatile personality. "Mary! Bring me my slippers," Grandpa Joe would erupt from the bedroom into the kitchen, where Grandma Freitas was cooking. "Go to grass Joe!" Most of the time, however, Grandma would fetch Joe's slippers without an unsympathetic word. Grandpa's irritability was understandable, as Joe, in his mid-sixties, when Thomas was eight, had undergone radical surgery for lung cancer in 1940—the result of a lifetime of smoking cigarettes and working at the Shell refinery for twenty-five years. After diagnosing Grandpa Joe with cancer, the doctors predicted that he would die. Joe did die at age 81, twenty-six years after his cancer was diagnosed and Thomas was twenty-four years old! Thomas remembers Grandpa Joe, as a large, cranky, gruff old man with a stilt-like gate, who walked around on crutches or was bed-ridden from time-to-time. Thomas knew that Grandpa Joe wouldn't hurt a fly, but Thomas would be on his best behavior, nonetheless. Out of the house, in his garage, Grandpa Joe flourished. He was a different person. Grandpa Joe turned into a Magic star. There in the garage, Grandpa Joe would take a wooden spool emptied of thread, a toothpick, a rubber band, and a chunk of wax and make tanks that moved slowly and climbed over leaves and twigs. Wow! That impressed Thomas beyond belief. Then, Grandpa Joe would cut a "V" shape piece out of the edge of a coffee can, attach the can to a long pole, and cut figs from the top leaves of the fig tree behind the garage—pure magic! Building racecars from wooden crates was another specialty of Grandpa Joe's. Grandpa Joe was O.K. with Thomas; and Thomas was O.K. by Grandpa Joe.

Religion and Child Rearing Practices

Parents in the 1800's through somewhere in the mid-1960's raised children in accordance with how they were raised and with how the Bible told them to raise children. As the United States roots were firmly planted in the country's soil, one can imagine that animal training practices were also employed to correct children's misbehavior—breaking the child's spirit was valued by many a parent. Whether brought up Jewish, Catholic, Protestant, atheist, agnostic, or in another faith, the rules seemed to be the same: children were to obey their parents without comment or question and children were to be seen and not heard. When these household rules were broken, the harsh hand of a patristic authority would ultimately enforce them. In the Judaic-Christian tradition Old Testament Bible scriptures supported the brutal treatment of children by telling parents that if they spared the rod, when bringing up their children, they would certainly spoil their children. One has only to read the Deuterocanonicals and Old Testament to find passages that encourage parents to whip their children often, if they love them. (Sirach 30.1 and Proverbs 13.24) The Old Testament tells parents that God is an angry, a jealous, and a vengeful God (Numbers 32.10, Nahum 1.2, Jeremiah 11.20) and that God becomes displeased and wrathful with his children's disobedience. (Numbers 11.1) God the Father burns his children, drowns his children, and turns his children into pillars of salt, when they are disobedient and anger Him. (Numbers 11.1, Genesis 6.17, Genesis 19.26, 2 Kings 19.35) The Bible tells parents that God the Father made all humans in His image and likeness. (Genesis 1.26, Psalm 2.7) Consequently, earthly fathers are only following in the footsteps of God, when they strike down a disobedient child.

The New Testament, however, presents a different, softer message for parents, seeking guidance in raising their children.

> "Children, it is your Christian duty to obey your parents, for this is the right thing to do. Respect your father and mother is the first commandment that has a promise added: so that all may go well with you, and you may live a long time in the land. Parents do not treat your children in such a way as to make them angry. Instead, raise them with Christian discipline and instruction. [Holy Bible, Saint Jerome Version (384 A.D.) Ephesians, Chapter 6, Verses 1-4]

There is ample evidence to support the belief that Phillip Greenstone was not a religious man or a man that believed in a steady diet of striking down his children, when they were disobedient. Phillip did not practice such brutality, when raising Sam; and, Sam did not use corporal punishment to raise Thomas. Phillip and Sam were humanistic and followed the more positive message of the New Testament: "Parents, do not treat your children in such a way as to make them angry." (Ephesians 6.4) As for Joe Freitas, Blanche's father, the disciplinary scene was more old fashion. While her father probably never struck Blanche hard, Blanche grew up fearing her father. Blanche, from all accounts, was a child that wanted to please her parents and did not push the envelope; but Blanche clearly used physical punishment to curb her mischievous rascal's misbehaviors, as Thomas did push the envelope.

The Domino Effect

If Phillip Greenstone was the American ambassador to France, Margaret Green-stone (Hurst) was the second cousin to the First Lady of the United States, Mary Freitas was from the upper-class of Portuguese society, and Joe Freitas was on the board of directors of Shell Oil, world events and the people who made them would have been riveting dinner conversation; and, the decisions made at the dinner table would have impact on world events the next day. But our story addresses the influences that world events make on the lives ordinary people, like the Freitas's and the Greenstone's (California version) who lived "normal" lives and raised six children: Sissy Greenstone, Sam Greenstone, Kenny Greenstone, Blanche Fretias, Joe Freitas IV, and Fred Freitas. What impact did world events have on the individual attitudes, thinking, and lives of these family members? And, what control would the Greenstone and Freitas families have on world events? To answer these questions, we will take a look at a relatively minor event in American history, an event, which set in motion a Secretary of the Navy, who became President of the United States, who changed the way government operated, which changed national policies, which created a middle class, which empowered ordinary people.

The night sky hugging Havana harbor was hot and humid on February 15, 1898 when a rumbling within the United States Battleship Maine erupted in a gigantic deafening blast that splintered wood and propelled twisted metal and men hundreds of feet into the night air. On April 25th the Congress the United States declared war with Spain. Assistant Secretary of the Navy, Theodore "Teddy" Roosevelt, immediately quit his job to help organize a cavalry regiment made up of cowboys, Indians, and eastern college football players to join the war against Spain. Teddy Roosevelt's "Rough Riders" sailed to Cuba to avenge the sinking of the Maine. Engaged in battle, the American forces were pinned to the ground by fierce rifle and cannon fire from atop a hill overlooking Santiago Bay. Faced with defeat and exhilarated by the din of battle, Colonel Roosevelt, a forty year old Harvard graduate and former North Dakota cowboy, rallied his regiment in a spirited counter-attack up San Juan Hill, routing the Spaniards and capturing the hearts and imaginations of the American people.

Several years later, Teddy reluctantly accepted the position of Vice President of the United States. Early in the fall of 1901, Roosevelt, who was taking a short holiday, was enjoying the wilderness deep within the Adirondack Mountains. Teddy's thoughts may have drifted to the early 1870's when his family had taken him, as boy of twelve, to this same area around Marcy Mountain. Teddy may have recalled canoeing through the Saint Regis Wilderness Area. He may have rubbed elbows with the Vanderbilt or Rockefeller kids with whom he would soon cross-political swords. Across the state, in Buffalo New York, Leon Czolgosz waited in the reception line at the Pan-American Exposition to meet President McKinley. Czolgosz's thoughts were singular. He raised his handkerchief-covered hand, which held a 32-caliber revolver, towards McKinley and snapped two shots into the President. McKinley's death marked the third assassination of a United States President within thirty-six years, a trend that disturbed the American people. After a week of searching the wilderness, Indian guides found Roosevelt and delivered the grave news. Thirteen hours after McKinley's demise, Teddy Roosevelt became the President of the United States. Teddy was destined to make an incredible impact on American history. An impressed and admiring Secretary of State, John Hay, described the new President as being:

> "Of gentle birth and breeding, yet a man of the people…with the training of a scholar and the breezy accessibility of a ranchman; a man of the library and a man of the world; an athlete and a thinker; a soldier and a statesman…with the sensibility of a poet and the steel nerve of a rough rider." [1]

After serving out McKinley's term of office, Roosevelt decided to run for the presidency. The American people admired Teddy and flocked to the polls, electing him the 26th President of the United States in 1904. Joe Freitas and Phillip Greenstone were among the seven million, six hundred twenty-eight thousand, eight hundred thirty-four Americans, who voted Theodore Roosevelt into office.[1] Teddy did not disappoint them, as he took on the flagships of capitalism, those rugged individualists that exercised unfettered power and untaxed wealth in the pursuit of more power and more wealth. Heretofore, men like John Pierpont Morgan (banking), Leland Stanford (railroads), Cornelius and William Vanderbilt (steamships and railroads), Andrew Carnegie (U.S. Steel), John D. Rockefeller (Standard Oil Corporation), and James B. Duke (the American Tobacco Company) and their progeny were stronger than the United States government. Before Teddy Roosevelt's election, the U.S. Congress, Presidents, and the rulings of the U. S. Supreme Court had endorsed a hands-off policy, respecting the voracious appetites of industry. After all, when industry prospered, so did the United States economy. But capitalism was a two-edged sword in a democratic republic. When the capitalist sword cut one way, the economic engines spurred the American economy to new heights. However, the back cut of the capitalistic sword divided the nation into two socio-economic classes—the very rich and the very poor. Teddy was the right president at the right time; and, the creation of a working class—a middle class—developed, as a direct result of Roosevelt taking on the corporate giants of his day. Without governmental restraints industrial monopolies would continue to slash wages for the white working slaves in the north and black slaves in the south. Cheap labor is a cornerstone of capitalistic enterprise. To suppress wages and capture cheap labor, industrial monopolies built towns to house, feed, and take care of workers, forcing workers to be dependent on company stores for food, clothing, and other household commodities at inflated costs, which were deducted from worker wages before they received their paychecks. Life for the American working class, including the Freitas' clan in California and the Greenstone clan in Kentucky would have been lived in poverty, if the robber barons' strategy had its way over President Roosevelt's battle for a "square deal" for every American.

President Roosevelt kept hammering on the industrial monopolies from the "bully pulpit" of the Presidency. Under his administration the heretofore poorly enforced Sherman Anti-Trust Act of 1890 was enforced by prosecutorial action of the federal government, which broke up large monopolies at alarming rates. Labor unions such as the Knights of Labor pressured industry in the work place. Investigative newspaper reporting brought the nasty industrial practices spawned in shadows boardrooms out into the white-hot light of public view. The combined efforts of government, labor unions, and the public press forced monopolies to reconsider their ways. Gradually Carnegie, Rockefeller, Stanford, and the like began to exchange their fierce masks of power and force for the smiling masks of philanthropy. The robber barons "got religion" so to speak. Carnegie, following his new belief in the gospel of wealth, committed ninety percent of his immense fortune to build Carnegie-Mellon University and underwrite the arts, education, and libraries through his foundations.

As we shall see, the standards of living continued to rise for the newly formed working middle class, which included Joe Freitas and Phillip Greenstone; and they lived to see their children, Blanche and Sam, benefit, even further, from the policies of Roosevelt and the continued expansion of industry coupled with wages, sufficient to raise a family and chase the American dream.

Blanche

On December 20, 1907, Blanche Mary Freitas was the firstborn and Brightest star of the Freitas family. Blanche was an intelligent and conscientious child, who grew up in the orchard and farmland areas in and around Walnut Creek, California. Around 1913, Joe Freitas III was born, but he died five months later. As the first-born daughter, Blanche carried responsibilities for helping her mother care for her brother and for the house. When Joe III suddenly died from causes unknown, a deep impression was made on Blanche. Later, when she gave birth to her son, Blanche was obsessed about the health of Thomas and proud of the fact that Thomas was a healthy baby.[n]

In time the Freitas's moved to 322 Warren Street in Martinez, California, where Mary Freitas gave birth to Joe Freitas IV (1915)[b] and Fred Freitas (1917).[b] By the age of ten, Blanche was the consummate help to her mother. There were five mouths to feed in the Freitas family, plus a house payment, which all came from one paycheck. Fortunately, Joe Freitas, Jr., benefiting from the Roosevelt's policies and the advent of labor unions, went to work for the newly opened Shell Oil Refinery in 1915. The Martinez refinery was America's first modern, continuous-processing oil refinery plant. It required only occasional shutdowns for cleaning and provided Joe Freitas, Jr. with a steady year round family income, which was augmented when Blanche went to work as an usherette at the Stage Theater in Martinez. Thomas recalls Grandma Freitas telling him how Blanche had selected and paid for most of the furniture in the house Grandpa Joe had bought in Martinez.

Joe Freitas Jr. joined the Martinez Chapter of the I.D.E.S. *(Irmandade Do Divino Espirito Santo)*, translated from Portuguese into English: Brotherhood of the Divine Holy Spirit. The missions of the I.D.E.S. were to serve the poor, conduct fundraisers, and organize the Martinez Holy Ghost Festivals. The Portuguese Holy Ghost *Festa* tradition dates back to the thirteenth century, when Queen Isabel distributed food to the poor and starving of Portugal. The story of the Holy Ghost Festivals captured Blanche's heart and imagination at an early age.[i]

As the legend goes, The Queen of Portugal, struck by the poverty in her country, would carry bread and meat in her apron and distribute it to the people she met in the streets. One day the King asked his Queen what she had in her apron. Queen Isabel said that she had roses. But this was winter; so, the King commanded Isabel to open her apron. When she did, roses fell to the ground. The King believed this to be a sign of blessing for the Queen's work with the poor. When a Mass was held in the Queen's honor, a dove—the sign of the Holy Ghost's presence—suddenly flew into the church and landed on the alter. Each year thereafter a Mass of thanksgiving was held in honor of the Queen. After the Mass, all of the village's children paraded through the streets carrying Queen Isabel's crown. Returning to the church, a parish priest chose one girl to be Queen of the Holy Ghost and gave special blessings to her and the people. A *Festa* of singing and dancing celebrated the event; and the public was invited for a free meal of *carne* and *sopas.*

The Portuguese Holy Ghost Festival tradition became the focal point of Blanche's young life. At seven years of age (1914) Blanche took part in her first Holy Ghost Festival at Saint Catherine's Catholic Church. She continued in the tradition for the next seven years. Whether crowned Holy Ghost Queen or serving as a court princess, Blanche looked forward to and proudly joined the annual festivals. From 1913 through 1920 Blanche attended grammar school, participated in Holy Ghosts, and helped her mother. She did not attend Alhambra High School, as the first-born and only daughter was obligated to stay home and care for her younger brothers.

In 1909, when Blanche was two years old, the motion picture industry was establishing itself on the Pacific West Coast. In that year, The Selling Polyscope Company opened in Los Angels, California and released *"The Heart of a Horse Race Tout,"* and movie houses in small towns and cities, like Martinez, began to mushroom throughout the United States. Blanche was a dreamer and aspired to be someone, who would, someday, be lifted above her circumstances. She was blessed with a bubbly personality, keen people skills, a superb financial sense, and deft organizational abilities. She had grown up in Martinez, knew everybody, and was very popular.[c] When the Stage Theater opened in Martinez around 1927, Blanche, age twenty, was in the right place at the right time—this would be her time to be lifted, albeit vicariously, above and beyond. She was hired, as the head usherette at the Stage Theater. Her job was similar to that of being Queen of the Holy Ghost—be attractive, be gracious, smile, play to the audience, and make sure that all of the other princesses and usherettes do likewise. Blanche, along with most Americans, was star-struck by the glamour and awe of Hollywood. Strong willed, liberated women like Greta Garbo, Norma Shearer, and Claudette Colbert instructed her in the arts of being a woman. Dashing leading men, like Lew Ayres, Clark Gable, and Gary Cooper, surfaced on screen, sweeping her off her feet. And, Blanche had a front row seat to it all. By 1929 movie house box office receipts hit $720,000,000.00 dollars per year, an all time high for the movie industry. And, when the Great Depression took its toll, the movie industry kept right on going because for a few cents people could escape for a few minutes from reality and be a part of posh and glamorous upper class or struggle with the down-and-outers to make it big by the end of the movie—the happy ending we all dream about.

During Blanche's short sixty-one-year life span, violence and wars were commonplace events. Presidential candidate Theodore Roosevelt was shot. while running for a third term in office. (1912) World War I broke out in Europe. (1914) The United States joined in World War I. (1917) World War II went into full swing with Blanche's younger brother, Fred, serving in General Patton's tank corps. (1942) The Cold War with the Russians threatened possible nuclear attacks at any time. (1950's) The Korean War (police action) began. (1952) Presidents Eisenhower and Kennedy's plans to invade Cuba failed in the Bay of Pigs. (1961) The Russian Cuban Missile Crisis was averted. (1962) President John F. Kennedy was assassinated in Dallas, Texas. (1963) American troops entered the Vietnam War. (1965) Reverend Dr. Martin Luther King, Jr. was assassinated in Memphis, Tennessee during the Civil Rights Movement. (1968) On April 3, 1968, Democratic Presidential candidate Robert F. Kennedy told the American public that violence, lawlessness, and disorder will continue to persist. "We've had difficult times in the past. We will have difficult times in the future. It is not the end of violence; it is not the end of lawlessness. It is not the end of disorder."[2] Forty-three days later Robert Kennedy lay dying on the kitchen floor of the Ambassador Hotel in Los Angeles, California, shot three times by an assassin. Ten's of millions of people witness the assassination via television.

Blanche was attractive, accomplished, and tough. She was, on one hand, a softhearted idealist—a dreamer—and, on the other hand, a hard-shelled realist. The crucible of conflicted influences, from presidential assignations and war through the roaring 20's, into the Great Depression, and the good life portrayed on the Silver Screen, strongly shaped Blanche's views on how life ought to be and ought to be lived. And, they shaped her hopes and dreams for the child that one day would come along in her life.

Sam

Sam Greenstone arrived, when America was the world's greatest industrial power. Science and technology were dramatically changing the everyday lives of people at all socio-economic levels. The future of the working class was brighter; and the economic slavery tactics were, for most of white America, a thing of the past. United States factory output was twice that of its nearest competitor: Germany. Science-based corporate management practices had replaced the iron-fisted approaches of the old robber barons. By 1913, the first management science was used to improve assembly line production at Detroit's new Highland Park Ford Plant. In 1906 a Model T Ford sold for eight hundred fifty dollars. In 1916 the Model T cost less than four hundred dollars. More importantly, Ford's assembly plant workers were the highest paid workers in the motor industry and the Ford Motor Company continued to make tidy profits. New science-technology driven philosophy permeated America's industrial scene and formed a belief system that rivaled religion. Corporate skyscrapers [41-story Singer Sewing Machine building (1908), Woolworth's 61-story edifice (1913)] overshadowed the spiraled-cathedrals in America and Europe, as new symbols of power and wealth.

The world into which Sam was born was in between wars, but simmering on low heat. Egyptian Premier Butros Ghali was assassinated. The Brazilian Portuguese Navies mutinied, as revolution spread through Portugal. There was the Bahia Coup, Persian Counter-Revolution, and the Albanian revolt were distant events from the Greenstones. At home, the Carnegie Endowment for International Peace was established. On the home front, Father's Day was first celebrated; and Philadelphia defeated Chicago 4 to 1 in the World Series. The United States economy was rapidly expanding, as were jobs for all Americans, as country was edging into the era of science and technology. Marie Curie wrote her treatise on radiography. Electric washing machines were introduced into American homes. J. J. Thomson first used positive cathode rays in a magnetic field to measure atomic mass. Charles Proteus Steinmetz warned the public about air pollution from burning coal and water pollution from uncontrolled sewage disposed into rivers. Murray and Hjort undertook the first deep-sea research expedition—and, let's not to forget the 1910 sighting of Halley's comet.

Sam Greenstone, the Enigmatic star of the Greenstone family, was born on May 28, 1910.[a] Although Teddy Roosevelt would lose his bid for United States President in 1912, the president and the man's colorful imprint on America would live on. What boy, reading about the life and times of Theodore Roosevelt, wouldn't be astounded? Sam was an early and avid reader. The personality of Teddy Roosevelt was the icon of the American male—intelligent, educated, athletic, intrepid, loved, feared, respected, rich, famous, full of humor and wit, a reader, writer, adventurer, hero of the underdog—a force to be reckoned with. Needless to say, President Roosevelt was the idle, the classic role model for every boy growing up in America. And, in young Sam Greenstone's eyes, Roosevelt loomed larger that life—a childhood idol, which, at some level, became an integral part his being. When Roosevelt died in 1919, Sam was nine years old. Thomas remembers his father talking about Teddy: the greatness of the man, the tragedies in his life, his accomplishments and interests, and his death. Sam was, in his own way, trying to pass on something from this great president to his son.

In 1912 Teddy Roosevelt and his son, Kermit, were back from safari, after bagging over five hundred animals in Africa—a feat politically incorrect for our day. He was mad as a wet hen at the fact that his former friend Taft's had gone soft on monopolies and had, in his estimation, mishandled the affairs of the

Office of the President. In fact, Taft was not an aggressive person. He was more of an intellectual, who did not like the political wrangling and hassling of the Presidency. Teddy went right to work, rebuilding his road to the Presidency. He threw his hat into the political ring by forming a third political party, the Progressive Party (nicknamed the Bull Moose Party). Roosevelt's opposition candidates were Taft, the incumbent President and head of the Republican Party, and Woodrow Wilson, a Democrat and former history professor and President of Princeton University. On the campaign trail the tradition of assassinating U.S. Presidents continued. (Excerpts from 10/15/12 edition of the Detroit Free Press)

"A desperate attempt to kill Colonel Theodore Roosevelt tonight failed when a 32-caliber bullet aimed directly at the heart of the former president and fired at short range by the crazed assailant spent part of its force in a bundle of manuscript containing the address which Colonel Roosevelt was to deliver tonight." "The assassin was standing in the crowd a few feet from the automobile. He pushed his way to the side of the car and, raising his gun, fired." "Schrenk, who is small of stature, admitted firing the shot and said that 'any man looking for a third term ought to be shot.'" "All this happened within a few seconds and Colonel Roosevelt stood gazing rather curiously at the man who attempted to end his life before the stunned crowd realized what was going on."

"Colonel Roosevelt refused to allow doctors to examine him at first. Later, doctors made an examination of the wound and announced, 'Colonel Roosevelt is suffering from a superficial flesh wound. Bleeding was insignificant.'" "Roosevelt soon traveled on to the Auditorium where he was scheduled to give a speech and told the crowd, 'I have just been shot...But it takes more than that to kill a Bull Moose...The bullet is in me now, so that I cannot make a very long speech...I want you to understand that I am ahead of the game anyway. No man has had a happier life than I have led; a happier life in every way.' "

Roosevelt's typified the tough stoicism of the American male, which Sam incorporated into his attitudes and behaviors; like Teddy Roosevelt, Sam faced life's ups-and-downs with a Roosevelt-like stoic manner: joking in the face of pain and death. Thomas can't remember a time when Sam gave any thought to pain. In 1971, Sam was smoking a cigarette while sitting on a pipe handrail behind the Alameda County Corner's Office in Oakland. He evidently lost his balance, falling on the parking lot surface below, breaking his scapula. Did Sam see a doctor? Oh, no. He couldn't afford to be immobilized and said that the shoulder would knit and be just fine. Although Thomas, who was thirty-one at the time, tried to talk his father into going to the hospital. The effort was futile. Sam continued to work as a freelance embalmer despite his broken shoulder. Within a few months Sam's shoulder sort of healed; and he went on a cruise around the world. Shortly after the cruise Sam died, alone in his apartment. Blanche had passed away in 1968. To this day Thomas believes his father knew that he was close to the end of his life, so why bother with a trivial broken shoulder and enjoy the life he had left.

As a youngster living in Long Beach, California, Sam played cowboys and Indians on the sidewalks around his house.[g] Sam, Kenny, his younger brother, older sister Sissy, cousins, and his parents would go to the Long Beach Pier for family outings.[d, h] One of Sam's favorite play spots was around the foot of Signal Hill, supposedly so named because Native Americans had used the hill to send smoke signals. By June of 1921 Shell Oil Company's Alamitos Number 1 well was producing more than a thousand barrels of oil per day; and Sam lost his playground. Signal Hill became the nation's most productive oil field, sending oil to refineries throughout the state, including the Martinez refinery.

In 1924 or 1925 Sam moved from Long Beach to live with his Auntie Esther[d] and Uncle Wallace Snelgrove. He would finish his secondary-school education at Alhambra High School in Martinez, California. Wallace was a local builder and contractor with connections who built bridges, buildings, and the Monument to soldiers of the First World War off the Monument Boulevard Exit to Concord/Pleasant Hill from Highway 680.

In high school Sam earned excellent grades and played quarterback on the football team. After high school graduation he returned to Southern California, attending the College of Mortuary Science located on the UCLA campus. In 1931 Sam graduated and passed the state's embalming license examination, returning to Martinez to work for Brunscher and Connolly Funeral Directors and Ambulance Service. Sam's stoic, unflappable-manner, and great compassion for others were traits well suited for the difficult and distasteful tasks that injury and death presented. Sam's stoicism fit the embalming and cosmetic preparation dimensions of his work. At the same time, his quiet manner conveyed great empathy to grieving families and friends. Sam involved himself in the community. He was elected president of a newly formed fraternal society in Martinez. And, as a Third Degree Mason of Berkeley's Blue Lodge, Sam coached new members through their initial degrees.

The wilderness seemed to reconstitute Sam's spirit. He was a duck hunter and an avid spinner and fly fisherman. Sam was very much at home in the mountain streams of the Sierra's. Following in the footsteps of Theodore Roosevelt with his

sons and John Muir, who lived in Martinez, Sam instilled his passion for the outdoors in Thomas by spending as much time as he could teaching Thomas to
appreciate and enjoy things of nature.[u]

Sam Greenstone's religious beliefs were shaped within the science-technology
culture of his times and a strong commitment to the welfare of others, as were the
policies of President Theodore Roosevelt and Franklin Roosevelt. Baptized in the
Congregationalist Church, Sam was most comfortable not talking about his
belief in God. Congregationalists believe that one's theology is personal and private—a matter to be kept between the individual and God. Sam was a quiet, private, and unimposing man of few words, an athlete, a reader, and
thinker—unfathomable at times, but sociable, well liked, and committed to serving his fellow man. Only once did Sam mention that he was an atheist. It really
didn't matter to Thomas, as he always saw Sam, as a gentle person, always ready
to help his fellow man.

Sam was good-looking, accomplished, calm, and introspective individualist.
His life was shaped by what he read, his life experiences, and by what he thought.
He cared about people and quietly demonstrated his ability to lead at school, at
work, and in the community.

Blanche and Sam

In 1923 Calvin Coolidge, "Silent Cal", was Vice President when Warren G. Har-
ding, one of our most naïve/corrupt Presidents, died. Silent Cal was President of
the United States for two terms. During Coolidge's watch, the prosperity of the
Roaring 20's benefited many Americans. Product advertisement spending flew
from 1.5 trillion dollars per year in 1915 to almost 3 trillion dollars per year in
1929. Fueled by nation-wide advertising campaigns, the American public bought
more new cars, tobacco, pipes, cigarettes, and more bright colored, sleek lined,
attractive packed products. Selling health and beauty, the Lucky Strike Tobacco
Company promised Americans, "Light a Lucky and you'll never miss sweets that
make you fat." In 1936, George Orwell quipped that advertising was the "rattling
of a stick inside a swill bucket." (*Keep the Aspidistra Flying*) Blanche and Sam were
two-pack-plus a day smokers. For that matter, Thomas Greenstone had been
smoking since conception, as Sam and Blanche's apartment and the family car
were constantly filled with a blue-gray haze of smoke. In one picture Blanche is
holding Thomas while sitting on the running board of a 1937 two-door Plymouth.[m] When Thomas was bigger, Sam installed a wooden back seat for Thomas so he could ride along and inhale clouds of second-hand smoke on all the
family trips, including their weekly back-and-forth rides between Oakland and

Martinez. Thomas's baby book shows his birth weight to be five pounds, five ounces. He probably should have weighed seven pounds at birth.

Not about to run for another term, President Coolidge wrote, "I do not choose to run for President in nineteen twenty-eight." The small piece of paper on which he wrote the note was memorialized in a Saturday Evening Post photograph.[3] Silent Cal was a worm trout fisherman of few words. Herbert Hoover took his oath of office, as United State's President in March of 1929. Hoover's campaign slogan, "a chicken in every pot and a car in every garage" won the day for the Iowa born Republican. In his acceptance speech President Hoover assured the American people that "the poorhouse is vanishing from among us." When Wall Street Stock Market crashed on October 29, 1929, most Americans were in the poorhouse, didn't have a chicken, a car, or a garage, and barely had a pot to piss in. Hoover assured the American public that "Prosperity [was] just around the corner." The depression deepened and Hoover was held responsible for the country's economic collapse. Hoover was mining engineer by training; and, his precise manner served only to distance him and his words of hope from the American public. His stand against repealing the 18th Amendment prohibiting the consumption of alcohol didn't win him any friends, either. Hoover was booed at a baseball game; after which the crowd rained down chants of "We want beer. We want beer. We want beer." Hoover ran for reelection in 1932, warning that if the Democrats were elected "grass will grow in the streets." Goodbye Herbert C. Hoover. Hello Franklin D. Roosevelt, the 32nd President of the United States. Grass didn't grow in the streets of America; but jobs and prosperity did.

Blanche and Sam married in 1934,[k] but the full effects of the depression, which were felt nation-wide, did not severely affect the newlyweds. Blanche's close friend, Mary Curtain, had married Virgil Caporgno,[o] whose father owned Caporgno & Company Mortuary located in Oakland. After the Caporgno's married, Mary and Virgil moved into a spacious, second story home in the mortuary that fronted Grove Street (renamed Martin Luther King, Jr. Boulevard). Sam was hired, as a full-time embalmer. Sam agreed to be on-call each night for removals in exchange for a small, rent-free apartment located on the second floor at the back of the mortuary. This working and living arrangement was the perfect hedge against the ravages of the depression years and the perfect nest for the two lovebirds. Blanche and Sam waited five years before things radically changed forever. In 1939, Thomas was on his way to form the Greenstone Triadic family constellation—mommy, daddy, and baby makes three.

Author's Note

Before moving onto PART II of our story, a comment about Dr. Thomas Zechariah Greenstone's name. Dr. Greenstone's family tree was firmly rooted in Kentucky. According to family lore, the name Zechariah is traceable back to General Zachariah "Muskrat Head" Taylor (1784-1850), who was the 12th President of the United States. Dr. Thomas Zachariah Greenstone has always wondered why he was named after a president who was quoted as saying, "On the subject of Presidency, I do not care a fig about the office." Could Thomas Greenstone's parents have wanted him to be inspired by this rugged, tobacco-chewing general, hero of the Mexican-American War, who had little schooling, no experience in government, politics or law, and who had never voted in an election? Probably not. Zachariah Taylor's presidency was short-lived. It was rumored that "Old Rough and Ready" had consumed tainted food, which led to gastroenteritis and to his death some sixteen months into his presidency. In 1991, Zachary Taylor's body was exhumed from its resting place and examined for traces of arsenic. While arsenic was found in his body, the results were inconclusive.

PART II

CREATION AND DEVELOPMENT OF A TRIADIC CONSTELLATION

"That in blessing I will bless thee, and in multiplying I will multiply thy seed as the stars of the heaven, and as the sand which is upon the seashore; and thy seed shall possess the gate of his enemies."
(Genesis Chapter 22, Verse 17)

"As some divinely gifted man, whose life in low estate began, and on a simple village green;
who breaks his birth's invidious bar, and grasps the skirts of happy chance, and breasts the blows of circumstance, and grapples with his evil star."
(Tennyson, in memoriam, lxiv)

Author's Note

Part II contains Blanche's account of Thomas's growth and development, which is typed in boldface Times Font to distinguish it from Dr. Greenstone's recollections of childhood, which are typed in italicized Times Font. The author presents the unabridged writings of Blanche and Dr. Greenstone's recollections of childhood. Consequently, the reader is presented with the actual facts and opinions that Thomas's mother wrote some sixty years ago, along with Thomas's contrapuntal recollections and impressions of those events.

October 4, 1939: a pregnant and joyful Blanche Mary Greenstone waits in the hospital to deliver her first and only child. Blanche begins *Our Baby Book* by memorializing the mothers-to-be, who shared hospital room 542.

Mrs. Margaret Stark and Mr. Willis Stark
Baby Collete Marie Stark, born October 4, 1939
Mrs. Stark left the hospital Saturday,
October 14, 1939

Mrs. Frances Gibbs and Mr. Owen Gibbs
Baby James Owen Gibbs born Monday, October 9, 1939
At 7:42 AM; Address 5420 Bryant Street
Mrs. Gibb left the hospital Wednesday, October 18, 1939

Mrs. Blanche Greenstone and Mr. Sam Greenstone
Baby Thomas Zachariah Greenstone, Born Monday
October 9, 1939 at 12:40 PM
Mrs. Greenstone Left the hospital Wednesday October 18, 1939

Mrs. Fitzgerald
Baby Clinton Edwin Fitzgerald born
Monday, October 16, 1939 at 1 minute past 1

Blanche's First Visitors to Providence Hospital: Johnnie and Charlene Fay, Grandma and Grandpa Freitas, Jean Freitas, Agnes Freitas, Mary Caporgno, Frank and Evonetta De Manty, Ida Howard, Kenny and Inez Greenstone, Mrs. Arnold, Eleanor Shonley (No visitors after 12th of October.

Congratulations and Gifts, Notes and Telegrams: Melba White (Mother's hairdresser and the girls from Melby Gray's Beauty Shoppe, Edith Citrino Vignaud, Josephine Seibert, Sis and Bill Brainard (Father's sister and her husband), Mrs, Arnold (flowers), Mary and Jack Connolly, Mr. And Mrs. Joe Maderios, Daddy's flowers, Mrs. Caporgno (flowers), Grandma and Grandpa Freitas (flowers), Harry and Adele Holden, Grandpa and Grandma Greenstone, Auntie and Wallace Snelgrove (flowers, $5 and $2), Loueff Harrison (Texas), Cigarette Man Bill (candy).

Gifts: Milne's Jewelry Store (fork, spoon, and knife), Johnnie and Charlene (Thomas's bathinette, kimono, and jacket, Frank and Dolores Salei (bath set and knitted coat and cap, Babe and Eleanor Shonley (knitted blue and white suit and cap), Mrs. Arnold (pink and blue knitted buggy blanket), Grandpa and Grandma Freitas (teddy bear, crib, kimonos, silk buggy blanket), James and Ida Howard (baby bunty). Joe and Jean Freitas (bassinet), Mr. and Mrs. Joseph Maderios (blue blanket), Winnie and Ray Rockwell (blue sweater and thermometer), Mr. and Mrs. Caporgno (baby buggy), Pa and Ma (baby crib, Aunt and Uncle Sylvester (cap, booties and coat), Mr. and Mrs. Gomez (blanket), Tony Freitas (brush and comb), Frank Souza (baby book), J. L. Silveria (white sweater), Carl Hendricks (baby book), Helen and Tony George ($1), Mary and Virgil Caporgno (a ring), Edith [Citrino] Vignaud (white shoes and socks), Josephine Citrino (pink felt shoes), Sis and Bill (bathrobe and booties), Johnnie and Eva Zunino (knit suit), Uncle Joe Valladoa (coat and cup of gagetries), Uncle Tony Valladao (coat and cup of gagetries), Mary and Jack Connolly (klienerts pants and toys), Marianna (blanket), Mrs. Bordoski (rompers).

The baby is named
Thomas Zachariah Greenstone
For his Daddy

Weight 5 lbs. 5 oz.
Eyes: hazel (blue at birth)
Hair: dark, later reddish brown (8/10/41)
Lashes: dark
Complexion: fair

Hazel eyes (blue at birth) and a fair complexion was important to Mom. Blanche always saw herself as a dark-skinned Portuguese—a "Black Portagee" in the racial vernacular of her day. Mom would tell me not to get a suntan because she didn't want me to grow up dark. Mom wanted me to become one of the white and beautiful people she saw on the silver screen. I was to be Mom's movie phantasmal incarnation of Lew Ayres, Clark Gable, and William Powell.

Everything Portuguese was to be put on the back burner. Blending in with the dominant American culture was essential for success. Although Mom understood and could speak Portuguese, none of the old country language and only small part of the old country culture (Holy Ghost Festivals, some foods, and a few Portuguese words) was passed on to me. Mom's emphasis on blending into the American "melting pot" was typical for the day.

Birth registered at Oakland, City Hall
Certificate reference number: 4139-1939

Baby Thomas's Birth Expenses Amounted to:

$ 103.00	Hospital extra week
85.00	Doctors
20.00	Housekeeper
21.47	Layette
36.00	Diet, weight, etc.
10.00	Vaccination
<u>15.00</u>	Circumcision
$ 288.47	Total

Discharge weight: 5-lbs. 10 oz.
"Baby Toby" delivered by
Dr. M. a. Torrano, Family Doctor
Nurses: Nadine Johnstone, R.N; H. Hertel, R.N.
Sister Elizabeth Ann, R.N.
Superintendent of Maternity Floor
N. N. Ashley, M.D.
Health Officer
Mrs. Beckman, Health Nurse
Regular Nurses: Miss Shonwald, Miss Nadine Johnstone
Miss Thomas, Miss Dolores Moe, Miss Carmella Sulli

OCTOBER 10, 1939—Thomas's favorite toy is a brown teddy bear.[P]

OCTOBER 25, 1939—First auto ride: Baby came home from the hospital. Mother gave baby Thomas his first bath.

NOVEMBER 14, 1939—Baby's first buggy ride. Thomas drank orange juice for the first time.

NOVEMBER 16, 1939—Baby really smiled for the first time.

NOVEMBER 19, 1939—First automobile ride with Thomas to Martinez. We got a flat tire on the way back.

NOVEMBER 21, 1939—Thomas had his first cold.

NOVEMBER 23, 1939—Thomas's first Thanksgiving

NOVEMBER 29, 1939—Baby really noticed for the first time a toy hanging from his bassinet.

DECEMBER 5, 1939—First time baby was out in the rain. We were on our way to the doctor.

DECEMBER 12, 1939—First time baby smiled a lot and wanted to play nearly all day. Laughed out loud: 9 weeks old.

Thomas had his first coughing spell. I'm so worried because he is only nine weeks and one day old and weighs 8 lbs. 7 oz.

DECEMBER 14, 1939—Baby played with rattle, 9 weeks and 3 days old and discovered me for the first time.

DECEMBER 17, 1939—Baby took first tub bath on Sunday.

DECEMBER 19, 1939—Thomas tried to roll from side to side and also tried to talk!

DECEMBER 25, 1939—Christmas: Thomas is 11 weeks old. First Melba White gave baby first Xmas present December 20th, blue bedroom slippers. December 23rd Mrs. Arnold gave Thomas two ducks and a fish. December 23rd Andy, Teddy and Jeanette gave Thomas a baby spoon and a toy necklace of large disks and beads. $3 from Grandpa and Grandma Greenstone and Auntie and Uncle Snelgrove; December 23rd sweater, caps and booties from Tia and Ti Tony. December 24th blue bathrobe and shoes from Johnnie and Charlene. December 25th Money from Jo, Sis, and Bill. $2 from Grandpa and Grandma Freitas. Money from Fred and Agnes. White shoes from Joe and Jean. Rubber doll from Grand ma and Pa Freitas. Rompers and rubber doll from Kenny and Inez.

DECEMBER 26, 1939—Baby carried on quite a conversation of goo's etc. Sure is cute. Tuesday started Baby's first bank account of $14.50.

JANUARY 6, 1940—Thomas discovers own hand and feet. They were sure a mystery to him.

JANUARY 17, 1940—Thomas took a nap for the first time sleeping on his back. Up until this time, he has always slept on his stomach.

Mom was a perfectionist. As the first born in her family she did everything her Mother asked her to do perfectly. She paid great attention to detail, as is evidenced by her meticulous writings, her pride in the fact that Thomas was a healthy baby, and her high expectations. High standards were learned at home and honed with every movie she saw—movie were Mom's idols, which were to worshiped and emulated.

JANUARY 20, 1940—Baby Thomas really took a good look at another baby, Francis Beetem, 15 months old—flirting kind of young—eh?

Mom was a flirt.ᶜ She dressed well and "kidded around" with anything in pants. She was brought up during the roaring 20's and was a flapper, a looker, and she dressed to the 9's...Blanche was the "it girl" "Boop-Oop-A-Doo" and "Oh, you kid." Mom loved and expected to be the center of attention. Being head usherette at the Stage Theater validated her worth; and she was delighted (at this point) to have a child as "cute as a button."

JANUARY 27, 1940—Danny is sure cute with Thomas. He keeps wanting to kiss Thomas; and keeps trying to reach Thomas's face. Danny is 5 months and 1 week older than Thomas; so Thomas is quite a mystery to Danny.ᴾ

FEBRUARY 2, 1940—Today Thomas ate cereal for the first time. He made faces, but ate it anyway.

FEBRUARY 4, 1940—He recognized Teddy Bear and played with it. Sure is cute.

FEBRUARY 8, 1940—Thomas knows how to shake hands.

FEBRUARY 9, 1940—Today Thomas is 4 months old and ate all of his cereal (1-teaspoon) without making any fuss. I guess he just discovered he could swallow.

FEBRUARY 26, 1940—Thomas had his picture taken for the baby show in April. Tonight Thomas's junior pottie chair, he was a riot in it and we nearly laughed ourselves sick. He was so cute.

MARCH 4, 1940—He looks at playing cards and how at 7 months also pictures and loves to tear paper.

MARCH 20, 1940—Wednesday, discovered two teeth at 11 AM verified by Mrs. A. Arnold. Thomas 5 months and 11 days old

MARCH 23, 1940—We discarded the bassinet and Thomas slept in his crib for the first time.

MARCH 26, 1940—Thomas had shoes and sox on for the first time in his life.

MARCH 27, 1940—Thomas used the pottie for the first time.

MARCH 30, 1940—Thomas's favorite toy is his Teddy Bear.[P] The bear is everywhere Thomas goes.

APRIL 4, 1940—Thomas held a glass of water and drank it. He spilled water all over the place, and he sure was cute.

APRIL 11, 1940—Thomas ate meat for the first time.

APRIL 28, 1940—Thomas fell off the bed while having one of his tantrums and we were eating dinner. Scared us nearly to death and cut our dinner short

"[H]aving one of his tantrums" implies that Thomas was having tantrums regularly. This leaves one with the impression that I was left to cry it out on my own at 6 months old. . "Baby tantrums" have a reason: hungry, left alone out of sight of parents-security issue, wet, rash, digestive problems…Who know what was going on? One thing for sure Mother was "high strung". She could not stand noise, especially from a baby that couldn't be silenced. And, Mom was one who wanted to be in control of everything—first born v. first born.

APRIL 30, 1940—Thomas ate a banana for the first time. Toxoid injection for Diptheria.

MAY 10, 1940—Thomas holds his baby bottle by himself.

MAY 13, 1940—Date of Baptism; Oakland California Godmother Mary Caporgno and the Godfather was Virgil R. Caporgno. Congregationalist Clergyman Rev. James B. Orr.°

MAY 18, 1940—Thomas crossed the Golden Gate Bridge, Bay Bridge, and rode the Ferry Boat for the first time in his life. Saw Edith (Citrino) Vignaud.

JUNE 1940—Thomas shakes his head back and forth when we said no! No! Too cute for words.

JUNE 1, 1940—Thomas's first vacation at Aunt Esther's Rainbow Lodge in the Sierra Mountains.ⁿ

JUNE 6, 1940—Gave Thomas spinach. He was eating it OK, but was making the darndest faces, so I tried it. It was so bitter I threw it away. I wouldn't feed him something I couldn't eat, so the next time I'll give him spinach it will be the fresh and not Gerber's Baby Food.

JUNE 9, 1940—Eight months old today. Thomas has 7 teeth.

JUNE 10, 1940—Thomas stood up by himself with the aid of his playpen (8 months, 1 day old). He tries so hard to talk more so than walking.

Thomas swallowed a piece of paper before I could do anything about it. I put him to bed for the evening on his stomach as usual he was fussing, so I slipped in later and he had turned completely over. Quiet an eventful day.

JUNE 20, 1940—Toxoid injection for Diphtheria; Vaccinated for Small Pox…Ten days have passed and has had no ill effects; very unusual so they say.

JUNE 23, 1940—Thomas did his business the first thing in the morning. Daddy would put him on the pottie and Thomas was thru for the day so for voiding he would do it when we put him on the pottie, but it is such a job that I would slip up on it.

JUNE 24, 1940—Thomas holds a glass beautifully, just as though he had been drinking from one all of his life.

JULY 4, 1940—Thomas's favorite plaything continues to be his Teddy Bear and pink and blue wooden doll toys.

JULY 15, 1940—Noticed Thomas creeping on. But we don't allow him to creep much on account of the locality.

Three possible reasons for the curb on creeping was (1) as the morgue room was just down the hall from the apartment, Dad walking into the house would track God knows what into the apartment; (2) pictures show me playing on the cement parking area behind the mortuary where there was a fair amount of traffic; and (3) we lived on the second floor and the kitchen door opened onto a porch and a flight of stairs leading to the sidewalk. [m, q, s, w, y]

JULY 16, 1940—At 9 and 1/2 months with our aid Thomas would take a step or two.

JULY 25, 1940—And now he gets around in his playpen at 9 1/2.

JULY 26, 1940—Dr. Torrano dropped in to see the baby when all of a sudden baby waived good-bye.

JULY 31, 1940—Thomas stands unassisted.

SEPTEMBER 12, 1940—Thomas (21 lbs.) climbs up in his play pen and reaches for things like car bumpers, steps, running boards to hold on to while he stands up.[q] Took Thomas off the bottle; No fussing.

OCTOBER 1940—Very good so far. Thomas never had any trouble teething. Thomas's a year old and has 6 teeth, 4 uppers and 2 lowers. Thomas has 10 teeth. He has been a perfect baby in cutting teeth, no trouble at all.

OCTOBER 9, 1940 BIRTHDAY: Today darling is 1 year old, and we are so thankful for such a good and healthy baby.

Charlene and I took Thomas to the photographer's, then we took snap-shots at my home. We dressed Thomas in a white knit suit, with red white and blue buttons. White shoes and white sox with a blue border. He sure looks cute. We think so anyway.

We had a birthday cake and, Thomas cut the cake. We also gave him a slice of the cake. He had a grand time eating it.

Gifts: Blue rubber elephant from Mother. White knit suit, climbing mon-key, and blue rubber duck from Charlene. Set of blocks $5, from Auntie, Wallace Snelgrove, and Mommy. $2 from Daddy. Woofy dog, rubber tank set from Virgil and Mary. Pink rubber hippopotamus, $1, from Janice. $5 from Pa and Ma. Card from Mrs. Arnold.

NOVEMBER 3, 1940—Started toddling today.

NOVEMBER 9, 1940—One year and one month Thomas walked all over the place by himself. We loaned his buggy to Dolores. Thomas 13 months old walks all over the house.

NOVEMBER 11, 1940—We took Thomas to Capwells to see Santa Clause. He looked at him as if to say, "So what?"

NOVEMBER 21, 1940—Thomas (25 lbs.) walks all around on his own.

DECEMBER 25, 1940—Christmas (1 year old, 2 months) Blue jersey suit from Fred and Agnes. White sweater from Joe and Jean. $1 Grandpa Green-stone; Wash cloth form Grandma Greenstone. $5 from Constantine. $3.10, white shoes, mittens and sox from Grandma and Grandpa Freitas. Red wagon from Virgil and Mary.[bb] Drum and Dog wagon from Charlene and Johnnie. Rattle from Janice. Rubber doll and duck wagon from Kennie and Inez. Sox from Mrs. Arnold. Rubber pants and bib from Aunt Anne. Box candy from Sam (Chinaman). Navy sweater, white shoes from Jo, Sis, and Bill. $1 from Ida and Howard and Xmas card and picture from Danny.

Some of Thomas's friends (1941-1945): Rita Bopp, 8 years old, played with Thomas (2 years old) nearly every day after school. Carolyn Eweing (quite a crush on her at 7 years old). Barbara and Betty (Mexican sisters), Carol Caporgno, Francis Beetem, Elsie Beetem, Coreen Peters, Paddy Smith (t), Mary Swanstrom, Danny Cameron (p), Bobby Whitney, Robert Caporgno, Leonard McNamara, Le Voy Wilkins, Herbert Soares, Eddie Nash Casada, Patrick Murry, Bobby Murry, Bernard Libergot, Richard Aquino, Henry and Leroy Lampkins (colored), David Saba, Percy (colored), and Erlean (colored).

JANUARY 6, 1941—Yesterday, Thomas picked himself up without any assistance. It was too cute for words.

Thomas at this time is the picture of health, and so many strangers remark about it. Certainly makes me happy, because I certainly do everything I can to make this so, and we're so proud of him.

Mother's hard work produced perfection (picture of health) and I draw the praise of others, which reflect positively on Mom. Blanche is bathing in the glory of a job well done. And, as a result my parents are proud of me. What will happen if things don't go according to plan and turn out less than perfect in the face of all of Mom's good intentions, best efforts, and good works?

He is just wild about Charlene. She wrestled on the floor with him, and he wrestles her right back, and he does love it. He certainly has a good time in his own little world.

And, when I take him for a ride in the buggy, he certainly thinks he is somebody.

P.S. A stranger predicted Thomas would be a Criminal Lawyer of an Ambassador…Hot dog! Only time will tell.

Expectations fly on the words of strangers; and, Mom cautiously basks in the glow of their comments.

When Thomas picks up any small article, he uses his index finger and thumb and his little finger sticks straight out.

I'm starting to break him. What a job. When he is on the pottie, it takes a couple of hours, nearly, for him to do anything, but just take him off the throne and it's bang-bang. What a job, as far as the other business goes, he is very good. He'll do it in the pottie every time, if we get up in time. Sure is nice Thomas has never been messy in that respect. Regularity certainly is a grand thing (in food, bath, play, etc.) and Thomas gets them all, and he responds very nicely.

JANUARY 7, 1941—Thomas is now 15 months old, and he really is a kick, never thought one could get so much pleasure from a baby. He discovers he can do things and does he get a bng out of it.

JANUARY 11, 1941—(K 15 1/2) months old and 30 lbs.) Thomas has to be put on a harness. He's so active. I'm afraid he'll run away or hurt himself.[r] Thomas got a red Radio Wagon from his godparents for his birthday.[bb] It was a big surprise and he fills it with all of his toys and wheels them around. He pulls Danny Cameron around in it too.

JANUARY 17, 1941—First haircut H. C. Capwells Friday, 15 months old, Thomas cried through the whole procedure.

JANUARY 23, 1941—Mary and I went to Mrs. Caporgno's for lunch, we played bridge later, and Thomas wanted to play too. So we sat him at the table.

JANUARY 24, 1941—Now, he is 15 1/2 months old. What a day, he ate Mrs. Caporgno's soap, etc.

JANUARY 28, 1941—We have been training Thomas for a week and although he has done well and at times given signals. Today Thomas did exceptionally well, he wet one panty.

Thomas's special hobby is throwing his bedroom slippers, toys, etc. out of the bedroom window.

Thomas gets a big satisfaction out of biting for some reason, and he is tricky. He comes up to you and makes off he is going to hug and kiss you, and then does his dirty work. If he sees he is going to get swatted, he just changes his teeth and hugs and kisses you for all he is worth, and then tries to bite you again, when one is off guard. What a rascal.

MARCH 3, 1941—Thomas is Almost 16 months old, we couldn't ask for anything more. He is a very good baby, eats well, sleeps well, plays well, and has a very striking personality, which we hope he will always keep and he was having a grand time when all of a sudden, he fell off the chair, the first time in his life.

MARCH 10, 1941—Thomas is 16 months and one day old. Today we let Thomas eat his own supper by himself, a little messy, but he got away with his food and drank his milk all by himself.

Ever since Thomas was 17 months old, he takes his soiled pants, sheets, or anything white he finds around the place, he puts it in the container, soiled or otherwise.

APRIL 4, 1941—Thomas is completely broken wetting his pants.

APRIL 6, 1941—Charlene and I took Thomas to the carnival, he cried because there was too much noise but cooled off some after a bit. Thomas won a panda bear, he picked # 15.

APRIL 8, 1941—Words can't express it, but to see Thomas do the hula is the last word. Mrs. Arnold can really make him go to town.

APRIL 14, 1941—Thomas at 1 1/2 years old is getting to be a problem child. In a cute way he strips himself of all clothing and throws everything out of the window.

APRIL 15, 1941—At 18 months old, Thomas is completely broken of wetting his pants. When he kisses you on his own accord, you can rest assure he is going to get into mischief. He has become a wicked throw. I guess he is going to be a pitcher. He throws his bunny from his bed clear out in the kitchen or anything he has handy he as done this for several months.

Thomas still has the bad habit of sneaking up behind people and biting them.

APRIL 18, 1941—Thomas loves to play with his cousin Steve in Martinez at Grandma's house.ʷ

MAY 14, 1941—Thomas is ill for the first time, temperature 104 and has tonsillitis. Dr. Samson, a woman, made a house call. The results of the fever, etc. show Thomas has the measles of all things.

JUNE 1, 1941—Wallace and Auntie Snelgrove have a cabin at Rainbow Tavern. Took Thomas to the snow. He loves it. He walks with us around railroads, mountain streams, lakes, and through the forests.ᵘ

JUNE 10, 1941—At 20 months old Thomas would empty the ashtrays and put them back in place. He has all the earmarks of being neat. I hope so, because his daddy is just the opposite.

JUNE 17, 1941—20 Months and 8 days old, Thomas's first three words together are "Daddy, all done."
Nearly every one who sees Thomas predicts he'll be a football player. He certainly is a mischievous rascal and keeps us on our toes.

The irony is that when I was old enough to play football, Mom wouldn't sign the consent papers because she was afraid I would get hurt. Dad had played football at Alhambra High School in Martinez and it was thought that he had injured his hip causing arthritis and causing him to walk with a limp the rest of his life. This did not stop me from playing unsupervised football games at the YMCA, pick-up games at Lake Merritt on the open grass area across from the Grand Lake Theater. There were more serious injuries in those games than on the high school football field; but there was no changing Mother's mind.

AUGUST 10, 1941—Sis, Bill, and Sam took Thomas to the S. F. Zoo.

SEPTEMBER 6, 1941—Kenny (Sam's brother) Inez, and Janice (age 7) comes to visit us. Thomas is almost 22 months old.

SEPTEMBER 16, 1941—We are having a time with him and his food, especially if it is something he doesn't care about, he just throws it all over the place or just tips his mush right over on the table. He just loves all kinds of vegetables. He's now 23 months old.

OCTOBER 9, 1941 BIRTHDAY: Thomas is 2 years old. We had a grand day. Thomas and I went shopping. After, he woke up from his nap. We took pictures and then Thomas played with Danny Cameron; then, we had Josephine, Sis, &Bill over to dinner. We all had little Halloween hats on. Thomas didn't know what to make of it with his birthday cake, etc.

Gifts: $1.00 Kenny, Inez, and Janice, Two picture books from Danny Cameron, $5.00 from Grandma and Grandpa Freitas, $2.00 from Auntie, Wallace and Grandma Greenstone, Blue kimono from Josephine, Aluminum plate and tooth brush from Sis and Bill, Polo shirts from Robert Caporgno,

2 pair of sox from Mrs. Arnold, $5.50 from Les toward a bond, a set of blocks from us.

OCTOBER 10, 1941—We let Thomas play on the mortuary roof. He loves to run around when I'm hanging clothes on out to dry. But when he falls, Oh Boy! He really has the skinned knees. He's so independent that he doesn't want help. "Mom, I'll fix it."ᵛ

OCTOBER 29, 1941—I took Thomas to the Stage Theater to see Mickey Mouse and Donald Duck. He was so excited, yelled and talked all the way through. People we're looking around and moving their seats, so, we left and Thomas started crying.

Toots is two years old now, and what a time I am having with him. He just loves butter, every time I step out of the apartment, and I can always depend to find him nibbling the butter, nearly every cube I put on the table has teeth marks on it.

Every time toots heard the tune, "I Don't Want To Set The World On Fire," Thomas recognized the song without the title being announced, he would say "Fire, Fire," pretty good for two years old.

And, Oh! Boy! What a temper when I get after him for doing something, he also would raise his voice to me. He can't carry on a conversation as yet, but in his own way, I bet he was telling me plenty and at two years old.

I can't remember exactly why Mom was after me that day, but I remember that I was gotten after a lot. It seemed that everything I touched in the apartment caused a battle. Mom wanted everything in its place and there was a place for everything. And, Mom usually got after me with swats, forward and backhanded slaps, spankings with coat hangers and slippers. After a while, Mom was beginning to reap the wrath of her own hand—I was well taught how to yell, rant, and rage.

Other times Mom would grab me by the wrist and put me in the dark closet, slamming the door as she angrily walked off. I remember sitting in dark on the floor of the closet with Mom's clothes, touching the top of my head, the sides of my face, and breathing Mom's perfume. I found the dark closet a pleasing punishment. Door slamming and hitting the walls with my fists became an almost automatic reaction during arguments during my teens. Parents are children's first and most influential teachers.

NOVEMBER 18, 1941 Thomas talks to everyone. His favorite people are the mailman, the Oakland police who lead the funeral procession, all of the people who work at the mortuary, and every person he meets.

WINTER 1941—Thomas has had colds and coughs constantly and ear trouble along with it.

DECEMBER 7, 1941 Japan Declared War on the United States.

DECEMBER 25, 1941 Christmas (two years two months old): Rocking chair from Grand ma and Par Freitas, Leather bedroom slippers, Blue horse with wiggly legs from Mommy and Daddy, Defense stamps: $1.00 worth from Grandpa Greenstone, Crayon set with book from Robert Caporgno, Hot Dog wagon from Rita, Fuzzy blue bedroom slippers from Fred and Agnes, $2.00 worth of Defense Stamps from Auntie and Wallace, Nook-Out Bench from Kenny and Inez, Cardboard book form Janice, ABC blocks from Danny Cameron, Army truck from Steve, Red, White, and Blue sox from Mrs. Arnold; Red and blue corduroy overalls, Tailor hat from Bill, Sis, and Jo, Wheel barrel and Jumbo acrobatic elephant from Charlene.

FEBRUARY 1942—Thomas is two years four months old and repeats everything.

FEBRUARY 25, 1942—Robert Caporgno was one year old yesterday. He is a cute as can be and Thomas loves him too. I'm sure they'll be good friends. Thomas is two years four months older than Robert and just loves to play with him.[x]

MARCH 1942—Thomas is two years five months old and wets his bed about once a week, pretty good for a boy so they tell me and at this age Thomas is a perfect roughneck.[s]

Thomas also pulled the teapot off the shelf because Sam had dropped his tie on it and Thomas pulled the pot and bonked him right on the head. He's is just into everything. We're just about to put him in reform school, God bless him…

At two years and five months of age it looks like the perfect little boy that attracted so much positive attention to Mom and the family has metamorphosed into a rough-neck that gets into everything and is headed to reform school. Things will never be the same and Mother's reaction spring from frustration and disappointment.

MARCH 10, 1942—Sam was taking a bath when all of a sudden; Thomas peed in his pottie and emptied it on Sam, instead of the toilet.

MARCH 21, 1942—First time Thomas stayed away from home over nite; he stayed with Sissy and I cried all nite. Sam didn't cry, but he was blue.

APRIL 1942—Thomas was completely broken of wetting the bed. He did it himself.

APRIL 18, 25, 1942—Thomas has a girl friend, Patty Smith, when we go to the mountains. Paddy is about 12 years old and the two of them play in the snow and go everywhere together.[t]

JULY 1942—At 2 years, 9 months, when I wash Thomas's face, he would say, "Go easy." Also, he recites "The Three little kittens". Sure is cute.

AUGUST 1942—Thomas says his prayers alone all by himself.

AUGUST, 22 1942—Mom dresses me up: tailored jackets and short pants with sharp creases; army, sailor, and air force uniforms, trench coats, and so on. I can't get these clothes dirty, but I always do and then, "Oh, boy!" Being the cute little boy all "dolled-up" by Mom was in conflict with the all-boy, roughneck image. And all of Mom's yelling and screaming, spankings and closet time wouldn't change me to her liking.[w]

SEPTMBER 6, 1942—Thomas is 2 years and 10 months, 28 days old. Thomas's 1st outing to the mountains and what a trip to the mountains.

SEPTEMBER 8, 1942—Janice, Thomas, Kenny and Inez, Sam & I went to Russell's Circus at Richmond.

OCTOBER 9, 1942—BIRTHDAY: Thomas is 3 years old. We went to Martinez with Thomas.

<u>Gifts:</u> $5.00 from Grandma and Grandpa Freitas, Sailor suit from Auntie and Mommy and Daddy, $1.50 from Auntie and Wallace, 50¢ from Joe Calton, $1.00 from Janice, Kenny and Inez, Football from Robert, Mary and Virgil, Bingo board from Danny Cameron, 10¢ from Johnnie Zunino, Telephone, broom, blocks, suitcase, picture from Mommy & Daddy, 3 handkerchiefs from Mrs. Arnold, $1.00 from Bill and Charlene.

At 3 year old Thomas's favorite foods, so far, are avocados and artichokes. A couple of Thomas's expressions, "Mommy, here me is." "You do dat like me does."

I was singing "Three Blind Mice" to Thomas (3 yr. 2 mo. old). He asked me to repeat the song and all of a sudden his lower lip hung down to his chin, his eyes filled with tears, and then he let out to crying. The reason was because the farmer had cut off their tails with a carving knife.

NOVEMBER 27, 1942—Thomas probably has the Whooping Cough.

DECEMBER 5, 1942—Saturday, my brother, Fred, left for the Army.

DECEMBER 25, 1942: CHRISTMAS: (3 years old) Fire Engine to ride, Fire Engine with ladder, Monkey, gun holster, cup, plate, spoons, book and crayons from Mommy and Daddy, $1.00 from Grandma and Pa Freitas, $3.00 to by train, overalls and stamps form Auntie and Wallace, Red Sweater form Robert, Sox and hankies form Arnie, Pajamas and toys from Janice, Kenny, and Inez, Ring toss game and village blocks from Charlene, Blocks from Church. Airoplane from Danny and Earl Perrin, Soldier suit from Sis and Bill, Sailor Suit from Josephine and Dell, Block Kraft from Danny.

JANUARY 26, 1943—At 27 months old, Thomas is breaking himself of wetting the bed. He repeats everything you say, but doesn't carry on a conversation as yet.

At 28 months old, Thomas can find the movie section in the paper.

FEBRUARY 10 1943—Thomas is 3 years, 4 months old. Today I was at Capwells and while I was talking to a saleslady, Thomas was talking to a little girl and all of a sudden he disappeared. I was frantic. I didn't know where to look for him. I asked the little girl where Thomas had gone, she said I think that way, so I headed that way, and as big as you please, her he comes walking out of the lady's dressing room. How in the world he ever found that dressing room had me guessing, although we had been there several times before in his young life.

Mom also took me by the hand into the morgue room to watch Dad embalm. While Mom and Dad talked the people on the embalming tables just lay still on their backs, looking up at the ceiling with their heads propped up on rubber headrests. The room was cold and the smell of embalming fluid filled the air. I would take off from the apartment and go to the morgue room at the end of the hall every day. Dad told me about the bodies and what he was doing; and he would let me help him—empty buckets, hold instruments, place parts in the "gut-bucket".

FEBRUARY 12, 1943—We took Thomas to the wrestling matches. Did he have the time of his life with a sailor there.

FEBRUARY 14, 1943—Thomas went to Providence Hospital with pneumonia ($45.00). At 3 1/2 years old, Thomas's favorite expression is, "Here we goes again." "Lue have a boy at home?" he asks people he meets.
He's constantly asking us, "Can I go over to Scotty's house?" That's where he goes and bums candy and oranges.

When playing outside in back of the mortuary I have to stay within sight of our upstairs apartment; and at the sound of Mom's voice I have to go answer, "Coming mother" (...just like Henry Aldrich in the Aldrich Family on the radio) and hightail it straight home.

APRIL 25, 1943—Easter Sunday Mom takes a lot of time dressing me up in white—white pants, white shirt, and a white coat. I have a tricycle with rear wheel fenders that helps keep some of the dirt off my clothes; but before long I'm getting a licking for getting my clothes dirty. Mother is fastidious about things.

My moving an ashtray from its place on the table, move any of the numerous knick-knacks from their places, or move the doily from its place on top of the radio when I'm looking at or feeding the fish are hanging offenses and a sure invitation to be swatted by a coat hanger or a slipper. If things go too badly, then it's the belt administered by Dad when he gets home.

JUNE 2, 1943—Mom, Dad, and I are down in Kern County California visiting relatives on their farms and ranches. I get to ride horses.[cc] They scare me when they bow their heads; but I manage to stay on when they lean over to eat the grass. All kinds of relatives on Mom's side of the family; but I don't see them enough to remember all of them, except for Joe Furtado, Baby Harlan, John, Andrew, and my Mother's Uncle Joe. Funny thing is I never get in trouble playing on the ranch; but then I'm dressed in overalls and Mom revels in the positive comments about me by the relatives.

JULY 1943—We have to stop letting Thomas go to Sunday School because all he does is fight.

There was a Welch Presbyterian Church on the corner of 18th Street and Castro (Now a gas station); on Sunday mornings, when I was playing on the block, the kids and music attracted me. So, as the family story goes, I wandered in and joined the party. Of course, my parents were unaware of my whereabouts.

JULY 9, 1943—Thomas is 3 years, 9 months old and I'm at my wits end. He runs away from us. Yesterday morning, he got up at 5:30 AM and made the rounds around the neighborhood. Mrs. Usher hauled him in about 6:15 AM. This all happened when we were sound asleep.

I liked to get up early in the morning and go outside. When I'm asked what I'm doing, I tell Mom that I was talking to my friends—the people sleeping in doorways and alleyways around the mortuary. They tell me stories and I love to talk with them. Mom worries about me but these guys won't hurt me. We just like talking. Mom thinks I'm going to be a politician because she says I sure have the gift of gab.

Today, I was washing clothes on the roof. He did the same thing again, he ran off. I was frantic. When he finally came upstairs again, I gave him a terrible licking with a coat hanger, that nite, when he went to bed, his legs were black and blue, and I was just sick all over. He just had shorts on at the time of the licking, and that must have been the reason for the marks, cause heaven knows, he's had several good ones. If this licking would of stopped him from running away, it would have been worth it, but a half an hour later, he repeats the same stunt. So I swear this will be my last licking, but I'm at an end, because he absolutely will not mind me.[v]

I have no idea why I continue to get in trouble. If I minded Mother, I wouldn't get a licking; but I love to run around and explore stuff. Yesterday, Mom held me and told me how much she loved me and that she was sickened when she hit me. I'm just a "bad egg" like she says; but I can't stay still and manage not to get dirty.

Thomas has absolutely no fear of anything. We took him to the carnival the other nite. Sam took him on everything, including the "whip" and the "airplane". He stood up in the plane and rocked it back and forth, with Sam

holding on for dear life. At 3 years and 9 months old Thomas sees the little cars they have for children his age as not exciting enough for him. What a life, I'm commencing to turn gray, and no wonder; he also has a terrible habit of spitting. Maybe it's just a stage he's going through. I hope so!

The Alameda County Fair is a blast; and I want to do it all, except for the kid stuff.

He loves classical music and music of any kind.

Music fills my soul and takes me to another world. I run, jump, and ride with the sound of music constantly running through my mind. It adds power and definition to my actions, from drumming my fingers and tapping my toes to jumping off rocks and cars, classical music lifts me to greater heights. While Mom has some appreciation for how music affects me it also drives her NUTS! When I'm listening to symphonic music, my head is in the radio speaker and it's a fight when Mom turns down the volume.

I believe a lot of Thomas's problems are caused from being tied up, and no yard to play. When we went to Merced on our vacation, he was no trouble at all. He was so busy playing, because underneath all of his mischief, he is very kind hearted and thoughtful.

<u>Thomas I'm writing all of this down, so that when you have children of your own, you will understand, I hope. No matter how much worry and trouble you have given us, we wouldn't give you up for all the gold in the world. Only because we love you more than anything else in the world, but you sure are a character and maybe some day you will be a great person.</u>

AUGUST 25, 1943—Ford Slapped Thomas.

AUGUST 1943—Thomas is a little demon. He buys his own cokes, has girl friends galore at the Riviera Restaurant. All the girls are his girl friends and he lets them know it too. There's Eleanor, Vivian, Katie, Lovely, Marie and when he sees them go into the Bar for their customers, he calls them on it!

At the Stage Theater, he has a girlfriend by the name of Betty. And, today, he stood by her for about an hour, while she was on duty; she introduced him to all the usherettes. He always goes up to the box office and asks if they have a cartoon of Mickey Mouse.

He shakes hands with the elevator girls. Curtains surrounded us, and he walks up to the man ands asks if they have any curtains that his mommy wants some. The salesman sends him over to the saleslady and the same scene is repeated.

He calls the men that check cars at Capwell's parking lot, "his men" and perches himself up on a high stool with them.

He also has a girlfriend in the music department at Capwells, and sits with her at the piano.

I'm forever chasing him as he is always running away from me to see his friends. He's so darn independent and has absolutely no fear of getting lost.

One day he walked up to the counter at Newberry's Store and perched himself on the stool by himself. In the meantime, two women sat on each side of him. The saleslady thought he was with one of the women and waited on them, ignoring him. When he noticed the other two women had been served and he was still unnoticed, he yelled, "Hey, I want a coke."

SEPTEMBER 6, 1943—The Boss and I had a run in over Thomas and the hole in the wall of our apartment.

OCTOBER 9, 1943—BIRTHDAY: 4 years old. We would have liked to have a party for Thomas, but the place doesn't allow it. No room, so parties will have to wait until later. Daddy had to go to work tomorrow (Sunday), so I will take Thomas to the show; Kenny, Inez, and Janice came over in the evening.

Gifts: Antiaircraft-Air Gun, Jeep, Paint books and crayons, Book about the Three Bears and the Three Little Pigs, $5.00 from Grandma and pa Freitas, $5.00 from Auntie, Wallace, and Mommy, $2.00 Defense Stamps form Robert, Hankie and cute card form Arnie. Bowling set from Janice, Bathrobe form Kenny and Inez, Picture blocks puzzle from Daddy and a handkerchief from Danny.

DECEMBER 23, 1943—Took Thomas to a church party and when Mrs. Jones said, "Now children let us all sing, 'Oh, Come All Ye Faithful'", Thomas was sitting in the front row said, "Mrs. Jones play 'Lay That Pistol Down Babe.'"

FEBRUARY 9, 1943—I am so mad at Thomas, Sam gave him a pocket watch a week ago and this very minute he is taking it all to pieces and is telling me he is going to fix it. He is 4 years, 4 months old. I don't know why he breaks everything he puts his hands on?

Mother didn't fathom the difference between breaking and analyzing something. I am an explorer, analyzer at heart; I wasn't destructive, I was analytical and curious. If the watch was so valuable, why was I given the timepiece at the age of four? Naturally, for such major crimes against the family, Mother's anger was to be assuaged by corporal punishment in the form of lickings or beltings; but my behavior never changed for long.

Last week I told him to shut-up his big mouth. He said, "Don't say that bad word Mommy." I said, "Well, then hush your big mouth." A couple of nights later, Sam and I were talking in bed, in the meantime he woke up to go to the bathroom, then got back in bed, and we proceeded with our conversation. He raised his head and said, "Will you please hush your big mouth, so I can go to sleep." That's our kid.

The butcher made the mistake of giving Thomas a hamburger. Well as you might guess, it turned out to be a habit. One day, I told him the other man was the butcher's boss and that the butcher couldn't give him any hamburger. Thomas told the butcher to tell the boss to go to lunch and then give him the hamburger. He got the hamburger.

FEBRUARY 25, 1944—Thomas attended his first birthday party at Mrs. Caporgno's for Robert.

Thomas can't pronounce his "V's", so for gloves, he says "globes."

When I'm scolding him, I'll say, "Why did you do that?" And, he will say, "Why did you do that?" He repeats after me instead of answering my questions. At this state I'm ready to pull my hair.

MARCH 16, 1944—Robert and I play a lot on the mortuary roof. One of our favorite pastimes is pushing puppies around in a basket weave baby buggy.[x]

MARCH 17, 1944—Thomas had his ears operated on. Ear lanced by Dr. Saam (female doctor) at Providence Hospital.

MARCH 27, 1944—I was sick in bed today and for Sam to kill time he decided to trim Thomas's hair, as the barber gave him a terrible haircut. While Sam was busy cutting hair, Thomas was busy cutting a hole in his pajama knee with the scissors, without our knowledge. The next day, when I was discovered the hole, which was as big as a dollar, I said, "Who in the world did this?" Thomas with a very innocent look on his face said, "A moth."

APRIL 2, 1944—Thomas's ear lanced again by Dr. Saam.

APRIL 10, 1944—Tonsils (tonsillectomy), adenoids & ears—$107.27 to Providence Hospital.

JUNE 4, 1944—Thomas, Robert, and Bobby Whitney playing with rubber gadgets they found in the back yard?

JUNE 14, 1944—One of Thomas's quirks is to put ants in a paper bag and take them to bed.
   Since Thomas has been 4 1/2 years old, he listens every morning to his favorite programs, which are: Don McNeil and the Breakfast Club, Cliff Arkett in Glamor Manner, Thom Brenaman in Breakfast at Sardi, and he tunes the programs in by himself on KGO.

SEPTEMBER 11, 1944—Thomas enters Kindergarten at Lafayette Elementary School (West and 18th Streets).

OCTOBER 9, 1944, BIRTHDAY: 5 years old.
   Thomas has a very bad cold. October 6, 1944 we had a dinner party at Mary and Virgil's. Bea Wilkins and us. Halloween decorations.
   <u>Gifts:</u> $5.25 from Mary, Virgil, Robert and Carol, $1.00 from Andy, Jeanette, and Teddy; $1.00 Kenny, Janice, Inez; Toss Game form Danny, $5.00 from Auntie and Wallace, Tank tinker toys, crow hunt game, books, areoplanes from Sam and me. $5.00 Grandma & Grandpa.

Thomas's secret at 5 years old is, "Nobody ever knows I have baby teeth."

OCTOBER 17, 1944—Mom was at school and took pictures of my friends and me.[dd] My friends looked like "Raga-muffins." Mother dressed me to the "9's" so I look like I fell out of Vogue Magazine—the shining white boy. Although the negros from the south were moving into West Oakland before and during the Second World War, we lived in the mortuary, apart from the changing demographics. Next school year, Mom enrolled me at Saint Francis de Sales School for the first grade. The streets where I played were mixed raced; but the Catholic school I attended was predominantly white.

OCTOBER 26, 1944—Thomas floored us this evening, when he sang the first song he learned in Kindergarten: "Choo Choo Choo, Choo Choo Choo, Every day the train will go, sometimes fast, sometimes slow, Every day the trains will go, Choo Choo Choo."

JANUARY 1945—Thomas is now 6 years old, he still has the personality and plenty of fortitude, but what a spoiled monkey.

Thomas's favorite toys are Guns, Bow & Arrows, Fighting.

Much of my make-believe playing involved violence and killing. I made little clay men and put them in the middle of the street to see if they can survive the cars going up and down Grove and 18th Streets. I love ants, beetles, bees, flies, and potato bugs. If I'm not putting them in a bottle to watch, I zap they with the death ray (magnifying glass) vaporizing them by focusing the sun's rays on them. I've killed a lot of innocent insects in fiery blazes or crushed inside of matchboxes place in the middle of the street.

FEBRUARY 3, 1945—Chicken Pox

FEBRUARY 8, 1945—Teasing Thomas that he is a girl, he says, "No, because I have fur on my arms." I told him to sit still in the car. He said he couldn't because, "the elbows in his coo hurt."

MAY 8, 1945—Germany gave up.

JUNE 23, 1945—Thomas lost his 1st tooth in Atwater on vacation.

AUGUST 14, 1945—At 4:00 PM we were informed that Japan had given up. Thomas is 5 years, 10 months, 5 days old.

SEPTEMBER 4, 1945—Thomas enters the 1st grade at Saint Francis de Sales School between 21st and 22nd on Grove Street.

OCTOBER 2, 1945—Thomas came home from school and said he had to belong to the Sunshine Club. The Club consisted of dipping his fingers in hot water, letting them soak to clean his fingernails.

He also said his row had the Bees, the row to the right the butterflies, and the row to the left the birds. Whenever Thomas draws, he never fails to make a sun or moon.

Recollections of kindergarten are all positive: playing, making friends, singing songs, eating graham crackers and milk, and napping. If I knew what elementary school held for me I would have stayed in kindergarten for the next eight years. Had academics been gradually and appropriately introduced in kindergarten, most kids would succeed in school; but such was and is not the case. In a blink of an eye kindergartners were expected to read, write, and compute proficiently by the end of the first grade. For the child that is "behind" for whatever reasons parents worry, teachers fret, and society laments and the child is stamped with some kind of label: "slow-learner", "special education", "disappointment."

OCTOBER 9, 1945—6 years old. Today we gave Thomas his first party. It was a surprise dinner party, with Halloween effects. Those present were Robert Caporgno, La Voy Wilkins, Lawrence Wilkins, Leonard McNamara, Mary Caporgno and Virgil and Bea Wilkins.

Gifts: 2 pair of corduroys, two shirts, flashlight, fire engine, a belt, $6.00 Auntie and Wallace, and $5.00 from Grandpa and Grandma Freitas. Howard $1.00, $2.00 Jeanette, card from Arnie.

NOVEMBER 2, 1945—We are having a terrible time with Thomas at school. He will not apply himself to studies, all he thinks about is play. Sister Stephen insists he is very intelligent and should be able to learn without much effort, but his little mind just wanders, his hard numbers are 5, 6, & 7. At home, he does very well with everything at present things look bad for promotion to the second grade.

Two months into the first grade things are going sour! Why won't Thomas learn—he's certainly bright enough to learn becomes the constant theme played by parents, teachers and me for eight years of parochial school years, then it really turns ugly in the ninth grade, but I'm getting ahead of myself in the story.

DECEMBER 1945—Brunners had a recording booth and Thomas heard his voice on record: "We're going to grandma's house this year, 1945, for dinner. I'm going to have a big juicy steak."

1946—This whole year Thomas's health is terrible.

Between inattentiveness in class and missing school for health reasons gaps in learning occur in mathematics and reading.

Thomas was asked, what could be bought in lbs. His answer was cantaloupes and watermelons.

APRIL 11, 1946—Thomas's foolin' around in class & kicked his shoe off, Sister Stephan Mary picked up his shoe & put it in her pocket.

I loved school. There were so many kids to play with. Mother walks me to school every day—down Grove Street, passed the Greyhound station, crossing San Pablo and Grove Streets to Saint Francis. Then, she lets me go across Grove Street by my self. Then Mom lets me walk alone from the Greyhound station. When she lets me walk to school, I can see her watching me until I cross at the "X" formed by Grove and San Pablo streets. I have to cross by the signal at Grove, then around the San Pablo Hotel to cross San Pablo Street by traffic signal, then along a row of shops between 20th and 21st Streets to school. By the end of the first grade I'm walking to school by myself.

MAY 1, 1946—Whooping Cough, Thomas's whooping cough lasted 24 days of constant throwing up; both of his eyes completely bloodshot.

MAY 4, 1946—Pneumonia

JUNE 14, 1946—End of the 1st year and passed to the second grade.

This was the next pattern: He's not learning, but he's so bright we'll pass him to the next grade on "trial promotion." This dance went on until the ninth grade.

JUNE 20, 1946—Thomas talked to the Andrew sisters, Paddy and Lavern at the Orpheum Theater.

JUNE 21, 1946—Thomas talked to the Andrew Sisters, Paddy, Laverne, and Maxine at Sherman and Clay. We had a record autographed and they gave him a picture.

JULY 31, Thomas fell on the sidewalk and cut his head, had stitches in the hospital.

Every summer the family vacation takes us to the mountains, Atwater, or the relatives' ranches and farms in Kern County.

OCTOBER 9, 1946—BIRTHDAY: 7 years old.

FEBRUARY 22, 1947—Thomas is 7 years, 4 months old. He has to be the BIG SHOT among his friends, giving orders, etc.

APRIL 24, 1947—We have quite a time with him. He almost refused to study, just wants to play all the time when he adapts himself his marks are excellent, when not in the mood to do things, his marks are terrible.

Took Thomas to Dr. Jean McIntyre, a children's dentist, for check up, he had an abscessed tooth and a dead nerve, it will cost us $65.00 to get his teeth fixed.

APRIL 26, 1947—Thomas, 7 1/2 years old, we crossed our fingers and let him go to the Kiddie Show at the Orpheum, all by himself, ye gads!

Saturday's at the movies are the best. Flash Gordon, Don Winslow of the U.S. Coast Guard, Sabu of the Jungle, Red Ryder and Little Beaver, King of the Kiber Rifles, Crimson Pirate, and plenty of cartoons—Mickey Mouse, Donald Duck, Goofy, Tom and Jerry, Elmer Fudd, and that crazy rabbit, Bugs Bunny—shown Saturday's at the Orpheum Theater on Broadway; and the lines are long. The entrance fee is 10 cents (although the Esquire is 7 cents) and popcorn is a nickel.

The Telenews Theater, just down Broadway off 18th Street, has great documentary films; and down stairs John K. Chapell broadcasts the daily news live over the radio. The audience watches him behind a plate glass window.

SUMMER 1947—*I have lots of toothaches. Mom says I will have three more months at the dentist to repair the immediate damage. The dentists said that when I have my permanent teeth, she would coat my teeth with fluoride, around 12 years of age. Fluoride treatments are a new scientific invention to prevent tooth decay.*

SEPTEMBER 1947—*Pat, the crossing guard, knows all of us by name. She usually takes me by the hand to cross Grove Street. She knows that if she doesn't watch us closely, we will start to run behind the Key System busses, becoming lost in the white billows of exhaust smoke. To this day I can still resurrect sensations of light-headedness and the intoxicating affects from inhaling the sweet monoxide as I run with my friends behind the busses. It's a miracle that we weren't brain-dead by the end of the* *second grade. Although I always suspected monoxide-poisoning caused Benny Candilaria's problems in Mrs. Clark's third grade class.*

OCTOBER 9, 1947—BIRTHDAY: 8 years old. It was a real surprise, as we had told Thomas he was to have no party, because we were broke and he was a naughty boy in school. We had a real birthday cake, white one with orange flowers to carry out the Halloween color scheme. Robert, Carol, Elsie, and Francis were present along with Bea, Maynard, Larry, Mildred and Helen. The party was given at Mildred's place.

<u>Gifts</u>: Gyroscope from Maynard and Mother, $2.00 Grandma and Grandpa, $5.00 Auntie and Wallace, Wrist watch, colored tinker toys, log cabin blocks, soldiers from us, Bird Bank from Bea, Brick Blocks from Carol and Robert, Giro plane Elsie, Puzzle Francis, Story Book Mildred and Larry.

Mildred and Larry Curtain were close friends of Mom and Dad. Larry was Mary Caporgno's brother and his wife Mildred was a nurse—always dressed in a white uniform and cap. I remember having a crush on her. She, like my Godmother (Mary Caporgno) was always so nice to me. Larry must have been six-foot four inches tall and he played with and protected all of us kids.

FALL 1947—Sam and I love going to the horse races every week whether it's at Tanforan, Bay Meadows, Golden Gate Field, or the races at the Pleasanton Fair Grounds. Thomas can't sit still with us in the box, so we let him run around the grand stands. Sometimes we catch a glimpse of him around the winner's circle, but most of the time he's somewhere playing. He has to check in with us every hour; and when he doesn't Sam looks for him. He has friends all over the place and earns money selling the San Francisco News-Call Bulletin. He loves to listen to Ira Blue announce the races live over the radio from the track, and every once in a while you hear Ira talking with this kid, Thomas—Oh, Boy!

Several times Sam found Thomas hanging around the track bars! Thomas would go up to one of the bars and place a dime on the counter and ask for a coke. The bar tender would either give him a coke for a dime or inform him, "I'm sorry son but cokes are two-bits." Sure enough some nice lady or drunk would throw two-bits on the bar and say, "Say bartender give the kid a coke." And, more often than not, they would give him a dollar of four-bits on the side. One day when the races were over Thomas didn't show up as he was supposed to. Then, we spotted him with some people crying his head off. Before Sam could reach him Thomas had stopped crying and arrived at our seats. **When asked what happened Thomas said that the lady had him pick horses and had promised him $20.00 to stay with her as a good luck charm but that the horses had lost, so she only gave him a ten-spot. He raised such a fuss that he got his $20.00 bucks. Some days Thomas goes home with more money than we do. What a con artist!**

After the last race, I'm running ahead of my parents to get to the car when this man in front of me falls flat on his face. He lies motionless as my Father checks the man's pulse. "He's passed away," was what Dad said.

Dad taught me how to embalm a body when I was seven or eight years old. He gave me his embalmer's manual from college and I would read from it. By the time I was ten or so, I knew most of it by heart.

A popular song was "Smoke, Smoke, Smoke." I still remember the lyrics: "Smoke, Smoke, Smoke that cigarette, puff, puff, puff until you puff yourself to death. Tell Saint Peter at the Golden Gate that he's gonna-hafta wait. I just got to smoke another cigarette." Mom and Dad were chain smokers (2 or 3 packs a day). The smoke cloud was so dense in the car on the way to the racetracks, Martinez, and on vacations that I couldn't see out of the front window of the car. They had built a small wooden bench/shelf behind the passenger's side front seat of the family 1937 two-door coupe.'" So, I was a second-hand smoker from age conception through fifteen years of age.

MARCH 28, 1948—We're having quite a time with Thomas, he just absolutely refuses to apply himself to schoolwork or anything worthwhile, except funny books, Kiddie Shows, guns & play of all kinds.

Play, play, play—Creativity, Escape, and Self-absorption…I loved playing inside the mortuary. Robert, Carol (Robert's sister), and I would run down the well-polished hallways and slide in our socks as far as we could, then with our feet running in place while we tried to turn the corner and run down the next hallway—great fun. Robert had a huge train set in the "Jew Room" where the Rabbi would sit overnight with the deceased. I loved to slide down the banister at night when no one was in the mortuary. However, one night I tumbled from the banister and rolled to the feet of a group of people talking after a rosary. They had been quietly standing at the end of the carpeted hall in front of the waterfall and fishpond when I rolled into them. When married, it dawned on my wife that I was that rude little boy that rolled to her feet, got up, and ran away when she was with her family at the mortuary—small world!

On rainy days Robert, Carol, their cousins, Elsie and Francis, and I would play hide and seek in and around the mortuary. My favorite hiding place was in the flower-wagon just outside and behind the mortuary, which was an old hearse.[y] Otherwise, we would play "trains" by pushing the baby caskets around the showroom and hallways or play hide-and-seek.

JUNE 11, 1948—Thomas's first vacation away from us. Today is the last day of school and tonight Thomas leaves at 10 PM from Martinez with Sissy for Davis Creek, near Goose Lake for two weeks vacation. Tuesday the 15th we leave for Hollywood Park for a week, then to Goose Lake to get Thomas.

Yes, I was sent on vacation to my Aunt Sissy and Uncle Bill's pig farm up by Goose Lake, right on the border between north-east California and south-east Oregon. Under clear blue warm skies and huge flights of Canadian Geese, I played in the creek that babbled along Sissy and Bill's home. This stands out as one of my fondest childhood memories. The dark side was that Bill didn't appreciate my energy level and inquisitive nature, interpreting my persistence in pursuing question after question about the farm as deliberate disobedience and flaunting his authority—the beginning of a beautiful power struggle. By nature Aunt Sissy was on the quiet and timid side, which was a perfect match for sadistic Bill.[aa] As the consequence of Bill and my failure to communicate, Bill would sit me in the kitchen on a white wooden chair where he could cuff me with his large heavy hand or grab and twist my ear on his way in and out of the house. One day, as a joke, Bill sent me with a bucket of feed to slop a herd of 300-pound sows. Things were going fine until I felt the sows eating the tops of my shoes. I was petrified with fear and crying when someone went into the heard and pulled me out of the crush of pigs. I can still hear the sound of Bill laughing.

I felt the rage ignite in my chest and spread to my face. I ran at Bill swearing and punching him. A few days later I was sent back home to my parents, but not before finishing my retaliation. I went behind the house to the tool shed, climbed up on the workbench, and grabbed a hand axe. Jumping from the workbench with axe in hand I landed on the dirt floor and still can see the dust rising around my feet from the impact; and ran into the creek with frogs jumping in every direction. I struck out at every frog I saw. A bloody trail of dead and maimed frogs laid behind me as I angrily hacked and whacked my way down stream. News of the massacre probably didn't get back to Bill, as I don't remember getting in trouble for that or for the small grass fire that mysteriously raged, but quickly died out just beyond the shed. No doubt I was the prime suspect, but nothing was said to me. My parents had to cut a couple of days off their vacation to pick me up. They were visibly irritated at, disappointed about, and apologetic for my behavior when they arrived. They were concerned about my uncontrollable flights of rage when "things didn't go my way." Sissy evidently told my parents about Bill's "picking on me" as the conversation on the way home revolved more around Bill and his abuse of Sissy that seemed to spill over to me, than about my angry run at Bill after the slopping the pig incident. Back home memories of the Davis Creek Massacre faded and life was back to normal—the usual yelling, screaming, and fighting.

JULY 20, 1948—Thomas joined the YMCA, 8 years old.

The Oakland Central YMCA was on 21st Street and Telegraph Avenue ᶠᶠ*, one long block from Saint Francis de Sales, which was at the other end of the bock at 21st and Grove Street. From ages eight through twenty-one I was cared for, provided job and leadership training, and given my first jobs by the YMCA. Gus McKinnon was the YMCA Secretary, who became a remarkable father figure for George Richmond and many of the poor waifs that came off the streets to play at the Y, including me. A gruff, no-nonsense, kind hearted Scotsman, all Gus would have to say in his Scottish brogue was, "Ah Thomas, why would you want to be doin' that?" I immediately felt ashamed and corrected my behavior to make Gus proud of me. Monday through Saturday I was at the YMCA and off the streets of West Oakland. I couldn't get enough of the Y. I learned to play pool, Ping-Pong, chess, checkers, basketball, football, track, weight lifting, trampoline, wrestling, slaughter ball, steal-the-bacon, and chase other kids around as much as they chased me. The highlight of every day at the Y was swimming.*

Down stairs was a four lane, 25-yard swimming pool, where we went for swimming lessons, free swimming, and later, swim team workouts and life guard training. Gus was also the YMCA swim team Coach. The ceiling above the pool was so low that a red spot was painted on it to remind divers not to spring so high. Eventually the diving board was removed as too many men and kids wound up bleeding and sometimes unconscious after landing face down in the pool. Interesting as no one wore swimming trunks at the YMCA. One lifeguard and several assistants were always on duty during the boy's sessions.

Once a month the Y had an afternoon outing for the kids. Y-guys went on trips to Berkeley Pier, the Oakland Main Library, parks, the movies, or the old standby, Lake Merritt. Then there were the Y-tournaments, tournaments for every age group and ribbons galore: Ping-Pong, slop-ball pool, chess, in-door track and field, and swimming. You-name-it and there was a tournament for it; and place ribbons were given for first through tenth place and everyone got participation ribbons. Our self-esteem soared. Just about every week, I showed off my ribbons to Mom and Dad, which brought them great pleasure and relief.

When I was eleven years old I was in the YMCA Jr. Leadership Program, and so was every eleven-year-old who wanted to be. We were proud to serve and to stay in the program we needed to be good examples for the younger kids. We were trained to checkout equipment to Y kids for the game room and gym. We were trained to teach swimming, assist organizing games, and to supervise tournaments and monthly outings. By the time I was fourteen, I was paid minimum wage as a game-room director, gym activities supervisor, and a Jr. Life Guard! I still got in trouble, but after the suspension or discipline I always had the opportunity to work my way back into leadership. The YMCA took the "long-view" with kids.

Swimming was my forte. I learned to swim at the YMCA. I started out at 8-years old as a Tadpole I, then a Tadpole II, and moved quickly through the ranks: Fish, Flying Fish, Shark, and then onto the Y Swim Team. At thirteen I earned my Junior Lifeguard Certificate. By fourteen I had earned my Senior Lifeguard Certificate, which allowed me to be a paid swim instructor, lifeguard, and swim team coach. I actually paid for my college books and tuition from the money I earned and saved at the YMCA. The Y opened their doors and gave me and many other kids the opportunity to learn, grow, and put our talents to use. The Y kept me out of trouble, instilled confidence and self-pride in accomplishing positive goals, and allowed me the opportunity to show my parents another side of my personality.

JULY 1948—Thomas went to the Oakland YMCA Camp located in Loma Mar.

Summer at Y-camp was another spectacular opportunity to grow and develop in a positive environment. As a camper, I thought I had died and gone to heaven. Breakfast, lunch, and dinner were joyous events: eating with cabin mates, laughter, singing, and games. Hikes, field games, crafts, archery, nights around the campfire, chocolate swims (night swims with hot chocolate with a floating marshmallow served afterwards), and the Ragger Society, a secret society for campers reaching the age of twelve who have been deemed "good campers" in the eyes of Raggers. A novice camper couldn't escape noticing that experienced campers and most of the adults had colored clothes tied around their necks: blue, red, gold, brown, purple, white...a square piece of cloth or some shinny material folded from corner to corner to form a triangle which was tied by a knot in the front, forming a triangular hood that hung down in back. And on the hood was a symbol of some sort: a cross within a triangle within a circle

One night I was shaken awake and peered into the beam of a flashlight held by my cabin counselor who whispered, "Come with me." Blindfolded, my hand was placed on the shoulder of a fellow camper and off we marched to Raggers' Point. Along the way the line of blindfolded campers were stopped by a voice in the dark, "Halt. Know ye not this is sacred ground?" Through the silent shadows we listened, as the story of the Ragger Society was told to us. Then, lead forward to the next halting place to hear more of the story unfold. At Raggers' Point we were helped to a kneeling position and sensed the flickering glow of candles that seeped around our blindfolds. The responsibilities of a Ragger were explained to us and the commitment to be true to the Raggers' Oath was made. Someone knelt in front of me, clasped my hands in the secret Ragger handshake, and told me the good behaviors that had been noticed, which lead to being brought to Raggers' point. I could hear the whispers of other conversations in the night. With the individual comments accomplished, the Blue Rag was tied around my neck as the person kneeling in front of me explained that the Rag was being tied was a square knot, which represented the "four square way of life" and which was never to be undone.

> *"Four things a man must learn to do*
> *If he would make his record true*
> *To think without confusion clearly;*
> *To love his fellow men sincerely;*
> *To act from honest motives purely;*
> *To trust in God and Heaven Securely."*
> *(Henry Van Dyke,* 1852–1933, American
> clergyman, educator, and author)

We were asked to remain kneeling to think about what was said. After moments of silence, a voice said, "You may now remove your blindfolds and stand." Looking up into the faces of those who had bestowed our Blue Rags a bond was formed.

I will never forget their faces lit by the glow of candles that accented Circle, Square, Triangle, and Cross symbols on the ground and the glowing undersurfaces of the redwood tree boughs, which formed a canopy over head. This was indeed a sacred and holy place.

The Ragger conducting the ceremony wore a White Rag and stood within the triangle of stone next to a cross of stones. Between the triangle and a square of stones stood red and purple Raggers, and between the Square and the circle of stones stood those with gold and brown rags. We were told the original Ragger Point had been located far upstream from the present location, but was burned in a forest fire. However, the stones, which lay on the ground were from the original Ragger Point. After the fire each of the stones was carried by a Ragger and placed in the exact position at the new site, as they were positioned at the original site. We were told that all Raggers may come to Ragger's Point to meditate and be with nature, but that the location of Ragger's Point and the trail entrance to the Point may not be divulged. After all the new Blue Raggers shook hands and exchanged welcomes, we all walked silently back to our cabins and slipped into bed.

At breakfast we wore our Blue Rags and behaved accordingly. Throughout the day I saw many of those who were at the previous night's ceremony: my cabin leader, the cook, a lifeguard, maintenance men—they were no longer just faces fast forgotten; they were respected brothers with whom I was connected.

Each summer I received a different color rag: blue silver, brown, red, and purple for being a "good camper" who, for the most part, upheld the values of the Ragger Society. In time I became a White Ragger^{ee}, which was a lifelong commitment to children and youth. I was privileged to conduct Ragger ceremonies and create the spiritual setting where other campers would receive their rags of various colors. The Blue Rag ceremony remained the best ceremony of all, as each initiate's face never failed to register awe and wonder when his/her blindfold is removed revealing the awakening of a deep spirituality.

Needless to say, summers at Y-camp were soul-enriching experiences that tended to counter-balance some of the trouble I got into at home and school.

SUMMER 1948—Sam took Thomas to see the Oakland Oaks play the San Francisco Seals in Emeryville.

That summer I heard music and laughter coming from the second floor of the white, gray trimmed Victorian house at the corner of 18th and Grove Streets. At night, using my parents' field glasses that they used at the horse races, I watched women dancing and playing. I don't exactly remember how I managed to get into their apartment the next day, but somehow I became their friend. I'd talk with these girls like I talked with my friends on the street, the waitresses at the Rivera Restaurant, my guy's at the parking lot, the usherettes at the State Theater, the salesgirls in the department stores, or the Andrew Sisters. Soon they would give me money and send me to the store to buy their milk, groceries, candy, and cigarettes (like I did for my parents). I'd fetch their hotdogs from the Casper's Hotdog stand at the corner of 18th Street and San Pablo Avenue. And, I would earn money for my efforts.

OCTOBER 9, 1948—BIRTHDAY: 9-years old. Celebrated on October 7, 1948 with a chicken dinner ($23.54)

For my birthday Dad had built a bicycle for me from the parts of several bikes. It had chrome fenders, a chrome chain guard, a black frame and a chrome headlight. It was the best bike I ever owned. I rode that bike into the ground. It seemed like I bent or broke the front wheel fork a hundred times. More than once I sheared off the waterspout sticking out from the side of the mortuary, as I turned too wide into the alley between the mortuary and the apartment house, next door. I'd crash into parked cars, other bikes, telephone poles, and curbs. I was a terror on wheels. But each time I brought the broken bike home, Dad would fix it.

Guests: **Robert Caporgno, Carol Caporgno, Bernard Leibgott, Patrick Murry, Bobby Murry, Richard Aquino, Eddie Casada, Benny Candaleria.**

OCTOBER 12, 1948—Sister Margarita Marie, my fourth grade teacher, heard me say "got darn it." She wheeled around and slapped me so hard that my teeth rattled and I saw stars. Sister then dragged me into the cloakroom and left me until dismissal time. After school I wrote, "I will not use God's name in vain" two hundred times on the chalkboard. As the man said when they strapped him in the electric chair and just before they threw the switch, "This has sure been a lesson for me."

At school and in church, when under the supervision of the Sisters of the Holy Names, the wrath of God was quickly delivered, especially to wayward boys. Slapping, striking the head or sternum with the knuckle of a forefinger, a piece of chalk, or a prayer clapper were the usual methods for regaining the attention of talkers, smart-mouths, and daydreamers.

The Saint Francis de Sales schoolyard was patterned similar to a prison exercise area with the Sisters/guards strategically placed throughout the space. The main playground area was visible from the second-story, west-end classrooms. The main playground was cement, except for the large asphalt strip beyond the end of the school and in front of the huge cyclone fence, and measured about ninety feet by 180 feet. It was bordered on the west and north by the school's two-stories of classrooms with push-out windows opening to the play area. The massive exterior brick wall of Saint Francis Cathedral sealed the south border of the play area. And, an imposing sixteen-foot cyclone chain linked fence closed off the east-end of the playground at the end of the asphalt. There were two regions of the playground that were tucked away from the main area and were out of direct supervision of the Sisters. The first section was a small, always in shadow except at high noon, play area beyond the tall iron speared gate leading to the playground from Grove Street, which existed at the bottom of the canyon formed between the school and the Cathedral. The iron-gate was supposedly locked during school time to protect the children from the world outside—we knew differently. The second area of relative freedom was on the asphalt around the corner of the end of the school. Lookouts were always place at the openings to the main school area to alert us when a supervising Sister was approaching. During my eight years at Saint Francis, the worst thing I witnessed happening in these cloistered pockets of darkness was one of the kids lighting a single match, which struck horror in the hearts of all the girls. That person, not me for once, was caught and had to sit, during recesses, on the bench outside the principal's office for a week. The dimensions and happenings of the playground/exercise area will forever be imprinted on the minds of the three-hundred or so gray and blue uniformed clad inmates/children who attended Saint Francis de Sales for eight years. Far from a dreary realm of existence, the playground was an exciting, happy, and adventuresome place for the most part.

I was often reported to the yard-duty Sister and was made to put my hand in her large, bottomless pocket and follow her around all recess. When she found out how much I liked that, sister just pinned me to her skirt. That was O.K. with me, as I enjoyed watching my schoolmates' whine, snivel, and lie when they were in trouble and brought before Sister. When I got home from school, my Mother would always know the worst that happened to me that day!

I always asked her how she knew all this stuff about me at school. Mother always answered, "A little bird told me." Then, Mother would take up where Sister had left off—out would come the coat hanger, spoon, slipper, or anything that was in arm's reach that would be used to make an impression on me. On occasion, Mom would call Dad to administer the heavy artillery. Dad was the last resort. "Sam it's time that Thomas be given a good belting." I would be made to drop my pants and lay on the bed with my bare legs dangling to the floor while Dad belted me three to five times. Afterwards I was in too much pain to be angry and couldn't argue or give excuses. All I wanted to do was to disappear for a while—whimper away in some corner of the apartment and cool my blistered legs and ass until the pain subsided. "Precious" needs a little time away to let the heat from his reddened legs and posterior dissipate into the atmosphere. But, I sure in the hell was angry with Mom. And I'm sure all the belting and beating fired the rage that welled up from within me during future verbal battles that took place between Mom and me.

Left to his own devises Dad approached child discipline much differently than Mom did. I do remember dad once hitting me when I lost a 50-cent piece in a theater; but such outbursts were rare. Rather, Dad would discuss matters with me in obtuse ways. He seemed to enjoy my creativity in attempting to match wits with him. Because I was always trying to protect myself from the corporal punishments, which accompanied my continual mischievousness, I was an accomplished liar, cheat, and all-around con man by the age of eight. Although I was forthright and honest by nature, truth was negotiable depending on the circumstances and avoidance of pain, blame, and/or shame that seemed to be a daily happening. Dad knew that he could only peal off the defensive layers by a non-threatening approach, which played on my inquisitive nature. Where Mom would slap me and said, "I said NO and this time I mean it" Dad would give me something to reason through to get the answer.

For example, I told dad that I was going outside and ride my bike. Dad said, "You'll shit a bug with a bell on it." Immediately I visualized a bug with a tiny bell somehow tied around its tiny neck, which was stuck in fecal matter somewhere in my colon. I next visualized my effort to expel the bug with the tiny bell as I was sitting on the toilet. I wondered what would happen to the bug when it hit the water? Would I have the heart to flush the tiny creature down? I wondered where would the creature finally wind-up? I pondered the probability of such an event actually happening. By the time I understood Dad's remark in relation to my statement I accepted "no" graciously; I wasn't taking my bike outside to ride. "Oh, OK Dad," was my usual response; and I went and did something else. Dad had given me a fascinating problem to solve instead of a rap in the mouth. I often as not left the situation amused and happy. The key was giving me time to settle down and accept the answer I didn't want to hear by amusing me with a clever mental puzzle to solve. The reward for the adult who did resort to the time-consuming, low-key approach was well worth their effort. After such an experience with such an intellectually engaging adult, I respected them and wanted to please them and conform to their requests. The problem was that these individuals were few and far between.

When I came home after school, I always was asked the classic question: "What happened at school today?" My response would be the classic answer: "I don't know." My attempt to avoid this question, at all costs, would frustrate my mom. Mom was not much for teaching by metaphor or old adages, although one of her favorite sayings was, "a little knowledge is a dangerous weapon." Her approach was to pop you one in the mouth, when she reached the boiling point. My Dad's response was, "I don't know got his neck broke." I would ask, "Give me some more candy, please?" Dad's response, "Tough titty said the kitty when the milk ran dry." Dad my foot hurts. "More than a square needle in your left nut?"

My friend Jerry remembers the time we came back from church. We both were in suits, our Sunday best. Jerry had wing-tip shoes on and I wore a pair of desert boots. We crossed the street and approached my father, who was cutting the hedges outside of the mortuary. Dad looked up and saw what we were wearing and said, "That boy would run around with his tallywacker hanging out if someone didn't tell him to zip up his pants." Jerry remembers my Dad's comment made over fifty years ago and it still sends Jerry into laughter to this day. That was Dad's disarming style:

"You'll find sympathy under shit in the dictionary."
"Don't take any wooden nickels."
"Got ants in your pants?"
"…like stuffing a wet noodle up a cat's ass."
"Balls said the Queen if I had two I'd be King."
"More trouble than Carter's little liver pills."

"...like scooping shit out of a barrel with a tooth pick."
"Don't give me that happy horse shit."
"Well, shit house mouse and apple pan dowdy."
"Now you want egg in your beer."

Dad had a million of them for every occasion, a little on the bawdy side, but that's what made them stick in my mind. By the time I was four I learned to visualize the spoken word, interpret similes, metaphors, as well as figurative and idiosyncratic language. I reasoned, problem-solved, asked a plethora of probing questions, and saw multiple-meanings in everything, which immediately captured the focus of adult attention. Best of all, Dad had established a great personal relationship with his son. If any of what I told Dad resulted in physical punishment, I would have learned how to further shade the truth; but none of what I told my father resulted in violence. If he told my Mother what I had said, which I doubt, I never heard a word. Dad had established a safe place for me that would last until I turned sixteen.

OCTOBER 26, 1948—I had to go to school and give Thomas a licking. My Gosh, when is he going to settle down, he'll drive me to drink.

The spanking in front of my fourth grade classmates the morning of October 26th was, as you can imagine, a deeply humiliating experience. I probably cried like a baby, to the delight of some of my classmates, but I can't remember. I have little recollection of the incident, but I', sure that after a while I erased the matter from my mind and went on my merry way. I do recall having more trouble on the playground during recesses at St. Francis because of my fighting. There were a bunch of bullies who picked on me until I started to fight back and retaliate. It didn't matter whether they could beat me up or not; I would go berserk and come away with some piece of them or wait and even with them in time. In my later grades I had only a few fights, as my rabid dog defense worked well to ward off the evil spirits.

NOVEMBER 1, 1948—Thomas is sure a bad egg when it comes to studying his schoolwork. Ye Gads!

This November was the first presidential election that made an impression on me. New York Governor Thomas Dewey ran for President of the United States against Harry Truman. My candidate was Thomas Dewey because he had a mustache like my Dad.

NOVEMBER 13, 1948—Thomas is 9 years old and attended his 1st football game with the YMCA boys, California vs. Washington State.

DECEMBER 17, 1948—My 4th grade teacher, Sister Margaretta Marie, assigned our class the task of doing a number of masses, communions, rosaries, prayers and visits to the church as a Christmas present for our parents. (NOTE: The following is the final product after many rewrites, which still contained punctuation and spelling errors.)

Dear Mother and Father,

Ever since the beginning of Advent I have been saying spencent prayers as my Christmas gift to you. On Christmas day when Jesuses comes into my heart. Holey comund I will ask him to bless you with his gressce.

Your loving child,
Your loving son you know how Ha Ha Ha Thomas

MARCH 7, 1949—Signed Thomas up with Scotty Weston Dance Studio for a 3 month course for $250.00. He loves his teacher, Maggie. Thomas is the only boy in the tap dancing chorus.

About all I can remember accomplishing was working my way up to the second line in the chorus with "East-side, West-side all around New York..." and "Shave and a haircut—six bits." When I left I had mastered the "bucking-wing" and was working on my "timing steps."

APRIL 4, 1949—We bought Thomas his first suit.

This evening Mother called me in from playing outside, "Thomas, Thomas, Thahhhhhhh-mas, Thahhhhhhhh-mas." Mom kept calling when she heard, "Thomas, Thomas, Thahhhhhhhh-mas, Thahhhhhhhh-mas" called in return. The more Mother called, the more she knew that I was mimicking her. When I finally got home she was livid because I wouldn't come in when she called and because I mimicked her. I was greeted with several good swats with Dad's belt and a tongue lashing, "Don't you ever do that again; you're making me look like a fool; and when you hear my voice I expect you here Mister. Do you understand?" Through my sobbing and crying I told her that I didn't mimic her and that it was the parrot down the street. "You little lying son of a bitch. I'm not buying your cock-and-bull story. Get to bed right now and no supper!" Several days later Mom called me; the same thing happened. She went down the back porch stairs and followed the mimicking voice. Sure enough on the porch of the house at the corner of 18th and Castro Streets, across from the Welsh Presbyterian Church was a parrot in a cage calling, "Thomas, Thomas, Thahhhhh-hhh-mas, Thahhhhhhh-mas." Mom felt so bad for calling me names and licking me that she cried and hugged me, apologizing all the way.

SUMMER 1949—During the summer vacation, we sent Thomas to a private teacher, Miss Lulu Wunderlich, at $1.50/hour.

OCTOBER 9, 1949—BIRTHDAY: Thomas is 10 years old.

I'm always on the go. My bike is part of my body; and I ride it everywhere: Lake Merritt, Lake Temescal, Lake Anza, the Southern Pacific Mole to go fishing, east Oakland, Berkeley, Alameda. If my parents knew how far away from home I was, they would have died of heart attacks. One particularly frightening mishap occurred when some other kid and I were riding down the road from the Caldecott Tunnel passed Lake Temescal. We were flying down the highway at break neck speed when my front tire slipped off the road into the gravel. The forces of the gravel stopping the bike threw me over the handlebars and into the gravel where I eventually came to a bloody stop. Nothing was broken, but my arms and face were shredded with blood dripping off the hanging pieces of dying skin. A motorist picked us up, helped clean me up, and took us home. I managed to have him drop me off in front of the mortuary; and when he left, I went around the corner and continued to clean my wounds out with water from the spout in the ally way and the towel the Good Samaritan had given me. I told my parents that I took a bad spill while riding through the parking lot on 17th and Grove Streets, which was where I was allowed to ride my bike.

Thomas has quite a mouth and swears like a sailor.

One thing, I didn't learn how to swear at school, home was the launch pad. It was easy to express rage through a string of swear words. As perfection was the expectation in my household, some vile explicative and an occasional violent outburst punctuated every event that wasn't carried off perfectly. Say I was playing alone and a tinker toy piece kept falling out of its connecting slot. "God damn, son of a bitch" and the piece would go flying across the room. Much of this behavior was learned at my Mother's knee, including the underlying rage at not having things work out as I expected.

My daily routine starts by waking early, dressing, making breakfast, and going to school. I usually have to stay after school for detention, to write sentences on the board, or to finish class work. I love writing with chalk; but I get cracks in my skin along my index finger from the dry chalk dust. Sometimes I get to bang the chalkboard erasers together and become covered with yellow chalk dust along with breathing the stuff. Afterwards, I walk a block to the YMCA where I get to play and swim until 5:30 PM. Then, I walk home, change clothes and play outside 'til dinnertime. After dinner I'm outside again. A little before dark, Mom calls me in. We fight over homework. We fight over my going to bed. We watch television. We don't fight during TV time. I'm usually asleep by 10:00 P.M.

Saturdays I ride my bike to the movies, then go to the YMCA. Sometimes I work Saturdays at Holy Names College, located across from Lake Merritt. Pulling weeds from the Sisters' garden is another form of punishment for my poor classroom behavior. Saturday night Mom, Dad, and I usually go out to eat. For some reason I behave well in restaurants. On Sunday I go to the nine o'clock Mass with my class. Later we visit Grandma and Grandpa in Martinez. Then, it's back home, TV, to bed, and up early Monday morning to begin the same weekly routine.

JANUARY 29, 1950—Thomas is the most destructive child with toys, especially with his clothes. No matter what he puts on his good or old clothes, there bound to be torn. Today he tore his good shirt. Last nite, I spent all nite patching, and he doesn't give a hoot. It's getting so we can't keep up with him. He won't study at school, everything is play and all he thinks about is fighting and guns.

One house over there is an empty lot covered with tall grass and rocks. It's a great place to have dirt bomb fights. The kids would break up into two armies and start chucking rocks and dirt clods at each other. All you have to do is pick up a handful of grass, and there would be a ball of dirt stuck to the roots. A quick overhead lob and the dirt bomb was on its way into the enemy lines. I still remember the feeling of getting hit in the head with a bomb and feeling loose dirt cascade down my back, into my eyes, ears, and mouth, not to mention feeling the loose dirt in my hair—great fun. One day the battle was raging fierce and kids from another block took up sides against us. They threw some of the cement rocks at us instead of dirt bombs. I counterattacked by hurling a big cement rock with both hands, backward over my head. The momentum of the throw planted me flat on my back, as I heard a blood-curdling scream. When I looked up I saw this kid holding his head as he ran across 18th Street. We ran after him only to find a trail of blood. We all split. The battle action had been so chaotic that no one knew who threw what; but I knew and kept my mouth shut. The next day I followed the trail of blood across the street and on the sidewalk to a house halfway between 18th and 19th Streets along Castro Street. I turned and went home. Evidently, the parents had contacted each other that night and that ended the dirt bomb fights, at least for a while.

MARCH 6, 1950—Thomas set the toilet seat on fire, nearly scared Mary and us to death.

Yes, I was at it again with my little clay people. I had built a toilet paper bridge from the roller across to the toilet seat opening to the bathtub. Clay guards were on and around the bridge. To escape pass the guards I burnt the bridge. I also ignited the enamel coating on the toilet seat that continued around the seat in bursts of flame. Mary Caporgno and Mom were having coffee and a cigarette just outside the bathroom in the kitchen. They weren't half as scared as I was. I don't remember the consequences; but Mary Caporgno, my Godmother, always had a kids will be kids attitude and often held in check my Mother's first reaction to kill me.

Mom didn't know the half of it. I was playing with fire every chance I got on the roof, in the mortuary, and in the back yard. A lot of things were going up in smoke around the neighborhood too: piles of dried leaves, newspapers, garbage cans, cardboard boxes, and the like. I almost burnt down the apartment house next door, but that's another story. I loved to watch fire burn.

Throwing gravel from the roof of the mortuary on passersby below on the sidewalks was a favorite pastime. Once I peppered a group of mourners' gather below who were sorrowfully waiting for their deceased loved one to be taken from the mortuary to the hearse. The door to the roof burst open and there stood one very angry Mother who chased me around the roof until I was caught and given a good licking.

Throwing things had always been a fascination to me. The ability to control the flight of an object and have it hit its mark was very satisfying and got me in a lot of trouble at home, school, and at the YMCA.

SPRING 1950: *Our Fifth grade teacher, Sister Roberta Mary, gave the class an assignment to write about our personal history. (NOTE: Punctuation, grammar and spelling errors have been left as they were in the original finished product.)*

HISTORY OF THOMAS GREENSTONE

My Childhood

One fine day in October a great blow struck my Mother and Father I was born. After about one month they took me home. I was very happy at the start, but as I grew older the trouble began. I contracted pneumonia three times and then whooping cough. When I was about three, I sat under the stove and a funny looking thing called a tie was hanging above me. I pulled it but what I did not know was that a teapot was on the other end. Down it came, they took me to the hospital I was quite used to it by know.

My School Days

When I was out of my youth I went to the first grade. There I met one of my best friends Pat Murry. Then when I was about in the third grade after school that day I wanted to take all my toys out side. That is where I made my first and big mistake! I slipped on the first step. Down I came, I reached the ground finally, got up and shook myself off. This happened about three times.

My Hobbies

When I was about five years old I was very fond of getting bugs until I was stung by a killer wasp. Then I started making model airplane I did not like that so I started leather craft. Then I went back to bugs, I had butterflies, beatles, ants, and grasshoppers. Now I disect fish. This I like.

My Future

My future is to be a laboratory technician. I like this because I wanted to be one when I was five. If I ever get out of grammar school this is what I will be. I hope to go to college and if I don't I can not be a laboratory technician.

By Thomas Zachariah Greenstone

Although my handwriting was labored, I discovered that I really liked to write. In the Oakland Tribune there was an Aunt Elise's page for young writers. The page was filled with kids poems, short stories, jokes, creative writings, and so on. Plus, the kid's name was printed under the story. So I wrote and submitted many stories. Finally one was published in the newspaper. This was an accomplishment that drew the praise of my Mother and Father.

JULY 23, 1950—Thomas went to Saint Mary's College for two weeks summer camp with Robert Caporgno.

OCTOBER 9, 1950—BIRTHDAY: Thomas is 11.

I was suspended two weeks from the YMCA for shooting a bobbie-pin into the lip of another kid, who was bugging me. The kid would hit me in the shoulder every time

I passed him. In the locker room he would snap me with a towel. So, when he chased me, I ran out of the YMCA Boy's entrance down the stairs to 21st Street turned and fired—right through his bottom lip. He bled like a stuck pig. And I was sent home for the longest two weeks in my life. Needless to say my parents weren't happy with me. To launch the bobbie-pin you take a rubber band, drop it over your middle and bugger finger, drop the bobbie-pin over the front rubber band, pull the bobbie-pin back, aim and fire.

Dad supervised my first embalming, an old woman. If word leaked out about my embalming a body, Dad would have had his embalming license suspended or worse. I was excited and full of question as I removed the lady's organs from her open chest and abdomen and dropped them into the gut-bucket. Dad took the woman's brain from her cranium, and we examined it together. Dad separated the sections the medical examiner had, which showed the brain tumor that had grown and taken her life. I remember Dad showing me the great wings of the sphenoid on the inside floor of the lady's skull. Oh, heart be still—head post and an autopsy for my first embalming—priceless! I rolled her brain in a pan of plaster of Paris (to absorb the moisture) and placed it back into her head. I replaced her skullcap and pulled back in place the hair covered skin on the top and back of her head, and tightly baseball stitched the skin flaps of her scalp together. At the same time Dad sewed up her abdominal/chest cavities in a like manner.

Dad was a quiet man. This was a remarkable quality as he was under intense pain all the time because of a degenerative hip joint, probably caused when he played quarterback at Alhambra High School. He was constantly taking pain pills and drank heavily. Every once in a while, however, he would explode. During supper one night, Dad, without saying a word, picked up a small can of Carnation half-and-half and threw it across the kitchen, breaking through the window over the sink. I guess he had had enough of Mom and my fighting. Dinner had a quiet finish that evening. Soon the fighting continued without further incidents from Dad. At the time I never noticed, but I'm sure my Dad simply withdrew further from the family squabbles as time went by.

Mom always gave gag-gifts to Dad. One was a picture of a yellow-faced man hiccuping with blue bubbles rising in the air. The man was holding a martini glass (an alcoholic drink supposedly created in Martinez, California) and had a stupefied expression on his face. The picture inscription read, "Drinking again Sam." Mom and Dad thought the picture was funnier than hell and hung it in the bedroom for months. I failed to see the humor.

Mother also had a gag—picture of me under Dad's picture. Well it wasn't exactly a picture of me exactly. It was a picture of a donkey with his head turned looking back at whomever was looking at the picture. A large fart cloud came out of Mr. Ed's rear end with my name written in the fart. That I clearly didn't think was funny. One night I made the donkey disappear. I knew Mom realized what had happened; but nothing was said. The next day I piled a bunch of leaves under a living room window that jutted out from one of the apartments and set it on fire. The Oakland Fire Department put out the fire; and I was never caught. I felt great relief watching the fire being extinguished by the firefighters.

MARCH 1951—*Some of the kids in my class pick on me during recesses. They grab me by the hands and feet, toss me between the church and the green lunch bench, and tried to crush me between the bench and the church. I would cry and get skinned up, plus the red brick would wear holes in my blue sweater and uniform shirt, leaving red brick stains on my clothes. Then I would get it when I got home for dirtying my school uniform. Eddie Casada had been one of my friends. He had been to my Birthday Party, but at school he joined with Barbarra brothers, two big fat eight graders, who used to chase and punch me every time he saw me. Calling him Barbara didn't help matters. I also went into my rabid dog frothing at the mouth act, which only invited more taunting and teasing. One recess Eddie held me across his lap, holding my hands behind my back, while one of the fatso brothers spanked me. I went nuts and bit Eddie's leg right through his salt and pepper corduroy pants. Eddie leaped up screaming; but I kept clamped to his leg like an alligator lizard. I heard from my father that Eddie's parents were quite upset and that Eddie had to go to the hospital for stitches and a tetanus shot. I not only escaped trouble at home, but also sensed that my father was amused by the whole incident.*

Later Eddie accidentally fell or was pushed down the stairs when the class was going out to recess. His momentum carried him through the glass windows in the exit doors. I heard that it took thirty-two stitches to close his sliced arm. Rumors flew that I had pushed Eddie. But Sharon Moffit, beautiful Little-Miss-Goody-Two-Shoes who saw the whole thing, never said a word. Eddie and the fatso brothers never bothered me again.

SUMMER 1951: *Some black kids were chasing me down the ally between the mortuary and the apartment house. I turned the corner not noticing I passed Larry Curtain (Mary Caporgno's brother who worked at the funeral parlor). Larry stood six feet four inches tall and grabbed the kids like a bunch of flowers. He dropped them one at a time saying, "Now it's a fair fight." The kids were just as scared as I was; and after* *an exchange of punches they ran away. The last one I caught with a two-by-four and he went limping away as fast as he could. Larry scolded me for not fighting fair.*

OCTOBER 9, 1951—BIRTHDAY: Thomas is 12 years old.

JANUARY 8, 1952—Thomas is in the 7th grade, forgot his manners in the cafeteria, and had to write the following note to his Dad to be signed and returned to the principal:

Dear Dad,

I was putting beans on the end of my spoon, and by hitting the other end I shot it up in the air in the cafeteria.

s/Thomas Greenstone

JANUARY 21, 1952—Thomas appeared on Bud Foster's TV Sports Show for writing about why he likes sports. His letter was picked as the best for the previous week's show.

MAY 1952—My classroom behavior was so disturbing that Sister Roberta Mary had me pick up my belongings and move into an empty classroom on the second floor of the school. The door was locked, except for lunch, and my assignments were slipped under the door. At first I reacted by tearing up my assignment sheet and throwing it out of the second-story window so it would float down like snow pass the window of my 7th grade class, which was right below. But, I adjusted and did my work and earned my way back into class.

SEPTEMBER 1952—I'm in the eighth grade and Mom is frantic that time is running out for me. I've been on trial promotion since the first grade; and Mom is afraid I will be in the eighth grade until I'm old and grow a beard, at least that what she told me.

DECEMBER 1952—Mom and my constant fighting and bickering has not subsided. Our three-room apartment was about 450 square feet of living space, total. The three of us shared one bathroom, one bedroom and a kitchen and living room. There is no privacy or breathing space for anyone unless we leave the apartment, which Dad and I do every chance we get. Mary Caporgno was a loving, compassionate, a generous Godmother, and life-long friend of my parents. She came up with the idea that I could move down the hall from the apartment to a room next to the morgue room and across from the elevator, which was used to store equipment, gurneys, and an occasional body or two when business was good. I was ecstatic. My mother was relieved. And, my father seemed to be my father. The fighting didn't end; but the number of fights per day diminished—out of sight out of mind.

Moving out of the apartment came at a good time as I had gotten into the habit of slamming the door and leaving the apartment every time I got real mad. I would storm down the steps and walk or run deep into West Oakland looking for a fight or as Dad used to say that his kid was "cruising for a bruising." I would walk down the street and position myself on a collision course with them. Usually nothing would happen, except for some name-calling and maybe some pushing. On occasion a fight would break out. I didn't really care if I lived or died at those times, so I fought as if I had nothing to lose. My rage was so intense that life didn't matter. I was lucky. This was the early 1950's when street fighting was with fists, boards, chains, rocks, and an occasional knife, but no guns. Deaths in the neighborhood numbered about two or three murders a year due to domestic violence. A few years later, I wouldn't have been so lucky: the Black Panthers of the 60's to the Ghost Town Boys through the 90's.

SUMMER 1952—*Somewhere during this time I met Jerry Guerino,[oo] who turned out to be a lifelong friend. I don't exactly remember just how we met, but it was probably at the YMCA. Jerry was two years younger that I was and marched to the beat of a much different drummer than I knew. Jerry didn't swear. He didn't have a chip on his shoulder. He didn't run the streets and fight. He wasn't angry and full of rage. He was athletic and the first nice guy from a healthy family that I recall ever meeting, except for Robert Caporgno. The Guerino family prayed before eating, enjoyed each other in conversation, enjoyed a good laugh, and accepted me unconditionally. The experience was powerful and drew me to them like a magnet. I adopted myself into the Guerino family with Louie and Cleda as parents and Jerry and his younger brother, Denny, as brothers—a home away from home. Decades later, Mr. Guerino told me of an incident that he had witnessed when my wagon full of newspapers toppled over and I began to "cuss a blue streak." With a smile and a laugh all he commented was, "Dag-blame it, I don't ever recall a youngster ever swearing like that in all my days." At the time no one preached to me or ever said a word to me about what to do or not* *to do. But their wholesome way of life set an example that positively influenced my behavior when I was in their house.*

OCTOBER 9, 1952—BIRTHDAY: Thomas is a teenager, 13 years old.

JANUARY 1953—I became a paid leader at the YMCA. My responsibilities included checking out and accounting for game room equipment (e.g., pool balls and sticks, Ping-Pong balls and paddles, checker and chess pieces and boards, basket balls, footballs, and softballs for the gym, and handing out towels after swimming sessions. One perk was several leaders were selected to represent the Boys's Division of the YMCA on a TV Quiz Show. The question that fate sent my way was, "In what country was the Winter Olympics held?" My answer was quick and certain, "Helsinki." The moderator said something and then repeated the question. I couldn't come up with Finland. To this day the embarrassment haunts me. But when that question comes up now it's, "Helsinki Finland" to the amazement of those around me—if they only knew the price I paid to have that correct trivia question answer on the tip of my tongue for the rest of my life.

MARCH 20, 1953—Thomas is absolutely a character in school, if he used his head for his studies like he does for his foolishness, he would be a genius. Day-in-day-out, year-in-year-out, same old story, study, study, study, and he fights all of us, but boy is he good with his alibis and excuses, and he has plenty of them. He is now in the 8th grade and we're all still after him to study.

I was in the house with the refrigerator door open guzzling a quart of cold milk as was my usual custom, when Mother entered the kitchen. She came unglued and picked up a broom and started hitting me with the handle until it broke over my shoulder. I'll never forget that liberating moment. I looked at her and realized that she had lost any chance of controlling me ever again. She slumped to the floor feigning some sort of an attack (…another ingredient of our fighting ritual, which usually resulted in our rushing to each other in an emotional embrace, ending whatever fit we were in—kiss and make up). This time I calmly stepped over her body and left the apartment, quietly closing the door behind me. While our yelling and screaming matches continued, Mom never raised her hand against me again.

Sister Mary Dorothea was my eighth grade teacher and principal, who only stood about five feet tall, but nobody messed with her. Although I had spent a lot of time over the years on the highly varnished dark-wood bench outside of the principal's office, Sister Dorothea approached me is a different and constructive way. She would stand in front of me with her folded arms hidden in her black cape and talk with me about what I wanted to do to help the school, now that I was an eighth grader. She found out that I wanted to work in the school store and that I was open to working on many of the school fund-raising drives that were held throughout the school year. I told her about what I did at the YMCA; and before I knew it, I was running the school store and organizing the school's rag drive, donut drive, and newspaper drive. She put me in charge of raising the flag on the roof of the school each morning and taking the flag down after every school day. I lost this privilege when I reverted back to my gravel throwing habits from the top of the roof, but I was simply asked if I wanted to take on the task of shopping for the best deal for an eight foot Christmas tree for the school. I still managed to get in trouble at school; but not like before. Sister kept the job opportunities coming—I was too busy to get into mischief.

APRIL 1953—Thomas does not mind us. We took him to deFermery Juvenile Hall, as he is incorrigible.

In those days parents could leave "incorrigible" children at Juvenile Hall for the weekend. Today, it's a different story. A child has to commit a crime (e.g., assault and battery of a teacher, bicycle theft, shop lifting…) to be placed in Juvenile hall. In any case, I liked Juvenile hall—caring adults, food, and games

APRIL 12, 1953—Thomas took "Michael" as his confirmation name. Thomas Zechariah Michael Greenstone, it was quite a day when the Bishop came to Saint Francis de Sales church.

JUNE 1953—My Lord, Thomas rewrote the story Dr. Jekyll and Mr. Hyde. Thomas performed his one act in front of the school, including teachers, priests, and Monsignor O'Donnell.

JUNE 11, 1953, 7:30 PM—Thomas graduated from St. Francis de Sales.

SEPTEMBER 15, 1953—Thomas enters the 9th grade as a freshman at Saint Elizabeth High School in Oakland.

OCTOBER 9, 1953—BIRTHDAY: Thomas turned 14 today.

OCTOBER 12, 1953—Thomas shaved his mustache.

NOVEMBER 1953—Thomas got a job delivering the Shopping News on Wednesdays and Saturdays. His route runs from Grove to Market Streets and from 3rd to Grand Streets.

What my parents never found out was that I seldom delivered the Shopping Newspapers because the newspaper boy on the adjacent route and I took turns burning them. After delivering papers for a week and noticing that most of the papers were never picked up, we decided that no one wanted the papers; so it was quicker to burn them in his backyard than deliver them. After a year of service, we received our one-year delivery recognition pins from the Shopping News for a job well done. I promptly quit the newspaper game (except at the racetrack) because pressures were mounting.

As we all know teenage years are turbulent. The first year of high school was located in East Oakland, far from where I grew up. After school there was a two-hour swim practice at the YMCA. For the first part of the school year I had two jobs, one delivering papers and the other at the YMCA. Mother and I still had our differences and screaming matches, but even that changed. . I actually missed the arguing routine with my Mother. It was the predictable pattern of our relationship that was gone. Mother would chew me out about something. I would explain or give some excuse. A screaming match would take place. I would slam the door on my way out. Then after a time we would apologize and tearfully embrace, vowing never to yell at each other again. For a while we were civil to each other. Even that was gone. Saint Elizabeth was not the cloistered environment that Saint Francis de Sales was. I knew no one. I couldn't understand the English, Latin, history, math and religion homework that demanded two to three hours a night to do, most of which was done halfway and/or wrong. Overwhelmed by feelings of inadequacy coupled with the reality of failure seemingly on all sides I walked home everyday after swim practice and shrank into the corner of my room. I would sit with my arms around my knees and cry or deal with panic attacks—I was cracking.

I continued to crack well into my late 40's, but I was productive, even successful, in the work world. Now, it is clear that my episodic panic attacks in adulthood were triggered by the same elements I faced in adolescence: the expectation to perform perfectly in the face of overwhelming feelings of inadequacy. In early childhood, my "striking" personality and rage in the face of criticism and other threats had masked the underlying wounds and despondency; but in time the façade crumbled.

APRIL 2, 1954—Thomas has Measles again. 14 years old.

APRIL 15, 1954—*My father was called by the principal of St. Elizabeth and was told that I wouldn't be able to return in the fall. The combination of huge learning gaps from elementary school, poor grades and terrible work habits had caught up with me. There would be no more trial promotions.*

AUGUST 1954—*The public high school for my neighborhood was McClymond's, which was located on Market Street in West Oakland. I wanted to go to "Mac" as my friends, including George Richmond from the YMCA, was a "Warrior." But my Mother didn't like George and certainly didn't want me to associate with the kids I got in trouble with in the neighborhood. It turned out that the mortuary's Grove Street address was in the Oakland Technical High School attendance area, so my parents sent me to "Tech." Jerry eventually moved out of West Oakland to attend Oakland High School. But George, Jerry, and I stayed connected through the Oakland Y swim team, the Oakland YMCA Camp during the summers, and Oakland Neighborhood Church. In point of fact both George and Jerry were good influences on me. They always seemed to use good judgment and were prudently cautious in street situations. I was the one that was the loose cannon.*

SEPTEMBER 1954—Thomas is a sophomore at Oakland Technical High School.

Tech is located between 42nd and 45th Streets at 4351 Broadway, a 24-block bus ride from the bus stop at 18th and Broadway, just three blocks away from my home. At the end of each school day I boarded one of the three key system busses waiting in front of the school and rode back to 22nd and Broadway where I got off, stopped at the Kwick-Way for fried chicken on a bed of French fries and a vanilla shake while on my way to the YMCA, which was right across the street. Although I still had the capacity to rage like a lion, my behavior at Tech was that of a lamb. I loved going to Tech; and did not get in trouble. Tech was a far away land. Few people knew me, and that meant my history and reputation had vanished without a trace, except within me. I went into a shell. I would walk around the school avoiding eye contact with classmates. I would turn and walk the other way if I thought that someone would say "hello" to me. The anonymity was healing, but fears and anxiety still continued. I perspired fiercely. Water cascaded down at the thought of speaking in front of the class or being singled out to answer questions. I spent a whole year in Mrs. McEntyre's Public Speaking class, giving only the introductory talk at the beginning of each semester. That first year I hung around with David Tanko, who I knew from St. Francis, and other kids from the ROTC (Reserved Officer Training Core) class.

SPRING 1955—After school I stepped aboard one of the busses in front of Tech and found myself struggling against the bus driver who was trying to get out of the bus with his money-changer and bag of tokens in hand. All I could think was here's a free ride home. I glanced to the back of the bus and I saw a fight with some poor kid getting the crap beat out of him while he was upside down in the rear exit well. I turned and sat in the bus driver's seat, somehow opened the rear door, letting the kid escape. He runs across the large pavilion area in front of Tech High and the back of the bus clears out after him. I went to the back of the bus, sat down at a window seat, and waited. The bus driver returned; and I got a free ride home. I never saw the kid that got beat up; but I made a point of remembering the guys that did the pounding. I guess they didn't recognize me, but I sure kept track of them. After that there were always several Oakland PD squad cars scattered around when school let out. For a time the Oakland police were hall monitors at Tech—Go Bulldogs!

I was surprised a few years later to recognize Huey P. Newton, the co-founder of the Black Panther Party, as one of the punks on the bus. All I can say is lucky me.

OCTOBER 9, 1954—BIRTHDAY: Thomas is 15 years old.

My straight A subjects were mechanical drawing and geometry. My worst subjects were algebra, history, Spanish and English. I liked biology, chemistry, physics, and ROTC, but barely got by.

I loved the military discipline and rewards system in my ROTC classes. I was on the drill team, the aggressor force, but only corpora, after three years because of my grades. No sports in high school, but I swam AAU on the YMCA swim team. I qualified for the Northern California Finals, which held at the swimming facilities at the University of California in Berkeley and competed in the Western Regional National's held in Phoenix, Arizona.

APRIL 1955—THOMAS IS 15 & 1/2 YEARS OLD AND IS IMPOSSIBLE TO HANDLE. HE ABSOLUTELY REFUSES TO COOPERATE. HE THINKS HE KNOWS EVERYTHING AND REFUSES TO LEARN.

I was shocked when my father got so mad that he grabbed me, tried to hold me against the sink in the kitchen, and attempted to knee me in the stomach. All I could think was how frail and in poor health Dad seemed. I guess my lousy behavior and the constant fighting with my mother finally got the best of him. I had no ill feelings over the incident, just pity for the quiet man that was my father. I also figured he was enti-tled to fly off the handle at me.

By this time I was a real handful to say the least. My Uncle Fred, who had served under Patton as a tank sergeant in the Second World War and was in one of the last tanks to get out of the Battle of the Bulge, was always the one who tease me and rough me up. One day he grabbed me from the back. I flip him over my back flat on the kitchen floor and stuffed him under the large preparation table.[5] In the process Fred got his nose broke as well as his glasses. As my Mother began to hit me, Uncle Fred yelled at her (from under the table), "Blanche, Blanche stop! It was my fault." Mother stopped dead in her tracks at the behest of her favorite brother's plea.

APRIL 25, 1955—Robert cut the legs off Thomas's baby chair. "Wow"

That kind of ended it for Robert and me. It was the last comment my Mother made in Our Baby Book.

MAY 12, 1955—I was Vice President of Palma Products, a Junior Achievement Company under the supervision of Oakland Tech. An awards dinner was held at the Lemington Hotel, and I had to say a few words in front of the gathering. It was one of the few times I spoke in public. I was shaky, but I didn't die. The Nordstrom Valve Division of the Rockwell Manufacturing Company sponsored our Junior Achievement Company. Our company manufactured these three-legged, painter's palette top shape tables. The tables were unsteady, but they sold. I received an award for marketing and sales.

SUMMER 1955—My friend Jerry invited me to his new church that his parents were attending, Oakland Neighborhood Church, which was adjacent to Castlemont High School. It was there that I learned to lead a different kind of life. The church had a large youth group that drew teenagers like the pied piper drew children through the streets of a town. Engaging, charismatic, larger than life youth pastors worked magic. Everyone who joined was wholly accepted, appreciated, and fully brought into the main stream of the youth group. What burdens were lifted from my shoul-ders—what a new life it was! I couldn't wait to get George Richmond to Neighbor-hood Church too. George was my buddy from Y camp and a purple ragger. Jerry, George, and I were all on the YMCA swim team, so we bonded together pretty well. Finally, he showed up and, from what I could see, found the church to his liking, although he kept his distance from the Omega group, but George was always a lone wolf.

Like the YMCA and Junior Achievement, Neighborhood Church was a place that developed leadership. As a high school junior, I was elected to be president of the Omega Youth Group, which was the high school wing of the church. Although I was shy at Tech, I was outgoing at church and the YMCA. I knew what it was to be ignored at the fringe of a group as well as what it was to be popular at the center of a group—both experiences benefited me in later life.

At fifteen I worked on the permanent summer staff at the Oakland YMCA Camp located near Loma Mar, California next to Memorial Park, a few miles from Pescadero and the ocean. I worked on the maintenance crews, clearing cesspools, removing poison oak from trails, building steps, cleaning toilets, and painting. In time I worked my way up to "Biffy King" the guy that cleaned and kept all the toilets running in camp. Being the "Biffy King" was coupled with responsibilities as a lifeguard, assistant cook, and being on call at all times. We would have Saturday afternoon and Sundays off, which was spent taking our clothes home for our Mothers to wash. YMCA work was six weeks long, but if one did their jobs well, they could work four weeks longer, as the Baptist Church Camp used the YMCA camp facilities while they were building their own camp across the creek. Everyone wanted the additional four weeks for the additional money and because Baptist Camp was co-educational—quite an incentive to behave and do one's work well. I qualified for four out of five Baptist Camp sessions. I missed one Baptist Camp because of a series of stunts like hunting deer with bows and arrows with my friend Norman Finley, running too many campers clothes up the flag pole, and being with the camp director's daughter at Raggers' Point when the toilets were overflowing one night. Boys will be boys.

GREENSTONE FAMILY TREE

John Thomas Greenstone
Born: ?
Place: Kentucky
Died: ?
Place: ?
(Married)
Alice Mildred Birdwistell
Born: ?
Place: Kentucky
Died: ?
Place: ?
⇓

Philip Mathew Greenstone   *(Married)*
Born: February 24, 1880
Place: Kirkwood, Kentucky
Died: April 24, 1942
Long Beach, California

Calvin Hurst
Born: October 14, 1862
Place: Tazville, Tennessee
Died: ?
Place: ?
(Married)
Caroline Purseful
Born   July 20, 1862
Place: Marrow, Kentucky
Died: ?
Place: ?
⇓

Margaret E. Hurst
Born: May 2, 1886
Place: Pinesville, Kentucky
Died: 1948
Place: Long Beach, California

⇓

Samuel Taylor Greenstone
Born: May 28, 1910
Place: Long Beach, California
Died: January 15, 1971
Place: Oakland, California
(Married)
Blanche Mary Freitas
Born: December 20, 1907
Place: Walnut Creek, California
Died: November 9, 1968
Place: Oakland, California
⇓

Thomas Zechariah Michael Greenstone
Born: October 9, 1939
Place: Oakland, California
(Married)
Marie Helen Castellanos
Born: July 10, 1936
Place: Jamay, Mexico
⇓

Kimberly Marie Greenstone
Born: January 16, 1967
Place: Alameda, California
(Married)
Jason Allen Adams
Born: September 6, 1970
Place: Fremont, California
⇓
Megan McKena Adams
Born: June 16, 2003
Place: Sacramento, California

Michael Taylor Greenstone
Born: October 9, 1968
Place: Alameda, California

FREITAS FAMILY TREE

Joseph A. Freitas, Sr.
Born: ?
Place: Flores, Azores, Portugal
Died: ?
Place: ?
    (Married)
Laura Mendonca
Born: ?
Place: Cavaida, Azores, Portugal
Died: ?
Place: ?
            ⇓

Antone J. Valladao
Born: October 14, 1862
Place: Flores, Azores, Portugal
Died: ?
Place: ?
    (Married)
Anna Rose
Born   July 20, 1862
Place: Flores, Azores, Portugal
Died: ?
Place: ?
            ⇓

Joseph A. Freitas, Jr.   *(Married)*
Born: October 12, 1883
Place: Alamo, California
Died: July 18, 1964
Place: Martinez, California

Mary Constance Valladao
Born: January 27, 1888
Place: Flores, Azores, Portugal
Died: May 24, 1973
Place: Martinez, California

            ⇓

Blanche Mary Freitas
Born: December 20, 1907
Place: Walnut Creek, California
Died: November 9, 1968
Place: Oakland, California
    (Married)
Samuel Taylor Greenstone
Born: May 28, 1910
Place: Long Beach, California
Died: January 15, 1971
Place: Oakland, California
            ⇓

Thomas Zechariah Michael Greenstone
Born: October 9, 1939
Place: Oakland, California
    (Married)
Marie Helen Castellanos
Born: July 10, 1936
Place: Jamay, Mexico
            ⇓

Kimberly Marie Greenstone
Born: January 16, 1967
Place: Alameda, California
    (Married)
Jason Allen Adams
Born: September 6, 1970
Place: Fremont, California
        ⇓

Megan McKena Adams
Born: June 16, 2003
Place: Sacramento, California

Michael Taylor Greenstone
Born: October 9, 1968
Place: Alameda, California

Record of Growth

Age	Weight	Height
One Week	5 lbs. 5 oz.	-
Three Weeks	5 lbs. 12 oz.	-
One Month	5 lbs. 10 oz.	-
Two Months	8 lbs. 3 oz.	-
Three Months	10 lbs. 5 oz.	-
Five Months	12 lbs. 8 oz.	-
Seven Months	17 lbs. 4 oz.	-
Nine Months	20 lbs. 4 oz.	-
One Year	23 lbs. 8 oz.	-
Two Years	32 lbs.	-
Three Years	-	-
Four Years	40 lbs.	-
Five Years, 1 mo.	47 lbs.	43 inches
	54 lbs.	-
Seven Years	54 lbs.	-
Ten Years	99 lbs.	-

Other Baby's Birthdays

Joanne Citrino, August 26, 1939
Stephen Dennis Freitas, April 29, 1939
Francis Lillian Beetem, October 17, 1938
Donna Shonley, March 3, 1936
Keith Jettie, October 10, 1939
Bobby, June 16, 1939
Robert Caporgno, February 1940
Carol Caporgno, July 2, 1943

Pets

Lassie, an Irish Setter*
Slicker, a German Shepherd*
Inky, a Chow
Sheba, a cat

* These were Robert and Carol Caporgno's pets, but I always considered them my pets too.

PART III

FINDING AND ORGANIZING THE PIECES OF THE GREENSTONE FAMILY CONSTELLATION

"Whoever inquires about our childhood wants to know something about our soul.
If the question is not just a rhetorical one and the questioner has the patience to listen,
he will come to realize that we love with horror and hate with an inexplicable love
whatever caused us our greatest pain and difficulty." [4]

"For now we see through a glass, darkly; but then face to face;
now I know in part but then shall I know even as also I am known."
(1ˢᵗ Corinthians: chapter 13, verse 12)

The study of what we know about Dr. Thomas Greenstone's early life will be approached in the same way one would study the development of a star or, say, the development of the sheep liver fluke, *Facsciola hepatica*—rather distantly and objectively. Just as one would identify, study, and understand the developmental stages through which an individual star or a sheep liver fluke travels, we will identify, study, and understand Thomas's developmental stages. We begin by describing twelve generic pieces of the human life cycle process (a process that applies to all human development) and by relating these twelve pieces to Thomas's individual development.

⇒ 1. The genetic-self: a unique combination of chromosomes ⇒ 2. Matures through biological driven developmental stages ⇒ 3. Raised, as their parents were raised. ⇒ 4. Learns by experiences ⇒ 5. **S**haped by interactions with nature ⇒ 6. Shaped by interactions within cultural-societal institution ⇒ 7. Shaped by interactions with others ⇒ 8. Thinks, wonders, questions, tinkers, learns, exercises free will, creates, and destroys ⇒ 9. Throughout life she/he has the capacity to shape or reinvent her or himself. ⇒ 10. May mate with another genetic-self. ⇒ 11. Creates/adopts or chooses not to continue the human life cycle until extinction do they part. ⇒12. Chooses to believe in God, Chance, or not to believe at all. (Please see next chapter for the discussion of the twelfth piece in Part IV.)

This down and dirty twelve-part generic model of the life cycle of a human in a nutshell allows us to reveal the key puzzle pieces of Dr. Greenstone's childhood experiences, growth, and development, and serves as the discussion framework for our story.

As humans, we are well aware that our human life cycles do not develop in a sequential and predictable manner. Consequently, one of the presumptions underlying our story is that random chance, chaos or Divine Providence (call it what you will) is the most dominant, ever-present force, which affects all life, including, of course, Dr. Greenstone's life.[5] It is not the author's purpose to argue religious-secular matters, only to acknowledge God's Hand or random chance's roll of the dice, as a profoundly significant dynamic that does declare a great invisible power in our lives.

For Dr. Greenstone, it is impossible to find the complete set of puzzle pieces, which would be used to recreate a flawless self-portrait of him, as a young child. For that matter, neither can we find a complete set of puzzle piece to form a crystal clear self-portrait of our lives. Because many of life's puzzle pieces were formed before we developed language, these pieces lie beneath our attitudes, behaviors and personality characteristics. In addition, isolating individual puzzle pieces is impossible because all of the pieces were formed within a complex and unique historical environment, which no longer exists and which has long ago become blended into the unseen, seamless foundations and inner structures of our beings. Scattered by time and clouded in forgetfulness, many key pieces of our beginnings will remain lost or blurred. Further, attempting to properly put our childhood experiences together based our adult memories of childhood will only give us a dubious or problematic glimpse of our past. This brings us to the second presumption for our story. By using all of the known information about our early childhood experience we can reconstruct a reasonably accurate portrait of our self, as a child and youth, regardless of the missing pieces and fuzzy nature of our memories.[6] Without this second assumption, none of us could approximate the beginning of our lives to better understand ourselves, others, and society.

So, what pieces of the puzzle do we have to work with concerning Dr. Green-stone's early life? *Mischievous Rascal* is based on five known sources of information. First, there is the baby book, *Our Baby Book*, which was recorded by Thomas's mother from 1939 through 1955. A second source is found in the hundreds of photos, which were taken of Thomas, his relatives, friends, acquaintances, and surroundings, during the late 1800's through 2004. Third, the impressions and observations of those witnessing the growth and development of Thomas and the current recollections of relatives, friends, and acquaintances serve us well. Fourth, we have several writings by or about Thomas from his early school years. And finally, we have the recollections of youth by Dr. Greenstone, the adult. With these sources in hand, we turn to examine the first of our twelve-element model human life cycle in a nutshell to witness the unfolding of our story.

The First Piece:
The Genetic-Self: A Unique Combination
of Chromosomes

Common sense, as well as science, tells us it is impossible to know when or what a newborn human is feeling or thinking.[7] Gazing in the eyes of an infant to understand her innermost thoughts and feelings, like gazing in the eyes of a cat to understand its thoughts and feelings, is a wonderful mystical experience, but pretty much one colossal waste of time. Accordingly, we will not go down the path, regarding Thomas's thoughts and feelings during infancy. But, in two years or so, we will come back to this topic, when Thomas's brain is a little better integrated and organized for expressive language. In the meantime, we will occupy ourselves with nine manifestations of Thomas's temperament.

Temperament

Temperament is defined as one's customary frame of mind or natural disposition.[8] The male and female parent chromosome contributions mingle to form the genetic blueprint for a new person, which is expressed by the little tyke within its first few weeks of life. Ogling parents eagerly note every behavioral expression and sound their newborn makes. The parents' responses to their infant's being and expressions communicate to the child the first impressions about communication within the brave new world entered. The newborn's verbal and nonverbal expressions, when experiencing and interacting with the world outside of self, are an expression of self, conveying to those around the child the mental disposition, spiritual courage or mood of the child.

Jon Winokur, the fellow who compiled and edited *The Portable Curmudgeon* disclosed that he has been in a bad mood since 1971. Clearly, that's John's customary or natural frame of mind. However, in our story the meaning of temperament takes on a special definition. Temperament tells us <u>how a person's behavior is transacted</u>, rather than what the behavior is or how well the behavior is accomplished. Imagine two boxers in the ring: equally skilled, the same height and weight, hands with lightning speed, as well as the same muscularity and strength. The fighters' temperaments may differ: How adaptable are the fighters in new situations? How much intensity can be brought to the fight? How persistent are the fighters in the face of attack? How distractible are the opponents? Adaptability, intensity, persistence, and distractibility are among the nine temperamental traits described by Dr. Alexander Thomas, Professor of Psychiatry, and Dr. Stella Chess, Professor of Child Psychiatry in their 1950 New York Longitudinal Study (NYLS) at New York Medical Center. Thomas and Chess identified three clusters of "temperamental constellations of functional significance" that described sixty-five percent of the children in the NYLS.[9]

The "Easy Child" accounted for forty percent of the study group:

> Characterized by regularity, positive approach responses to new stimuli, high adaptability to change and mild or moderately intense mood, which is preponderantly positive. These children are quick to develop regular sleep and feeding schedules, take to most new foods easily, smile at strangers, adapt easily to new school, accept most frustration with little fuss, and accept the rules of new games with no trouble. Such a youngster is aptly called the Easy Child, and is usually a joy to his parents, pediatricians, and teachers.

The "Slow-to-Warm-up Child" made up fifteen percent of the study population.

> Negative responses of mild intensity to new stimuli with slow adaptability after repeated contact; and show mild intensity of reactions, whether positive or negative, and by less tendency to show irregularity of biological functions. The negative mild responses to new stimuli can be seen in the first encounter with the bath, a new food, a new place or a new school situation. If given the opportunity to re-experience such new situations over time and without pressure, such a child gradually comes to show a positive interest and involvement.

The "Difficult Child" comprised ten percent of the study.

> Irregularity in biological functions, negative withdrawal responses to new stimuli, non-adaptability or slow adaptability to change, and intense mood expressions, which are frequently negative. These children show irregular sleep and feeding schedules, slow acceptance of new foods, prolonged adjustment periods to new routines, people, or situations, and relatively frequent and loud periods of crying. Laughter, also, is characteristically loud. Frustration typically produces a violent tantrum.

The remaining thirty-five percent of the children did not squarely fit into any of the three temperamental clusters. Rather, their temperaments reflected different combinations of the nine identified temperamental traits defined by Thomas and Chess.[10] Given Thomas and Chess's research, our threshold question becomes into which temperamental clusters did Thomas fit? To answer that question we must understand Thomas's temperamental behaviors as seen through the eyes of Blanche, an ogling parent who eagerly recorded every behavioral expression Thomas made.

The First 12 Months

Blanche recorded sixty-two observations and made twenty-four comments about Thomas's life, during his first year that fell into sixteen broad areas.

> Auto rides, being touched, changes in routine, creeping-standing-walking, eating, hand dexterity, gross body movements, playing with toys, potty training, reactions to new situations, communicating, sleeping-napping, smiling and laughing, tantrums, teething, watching and examining, and wearing cloths.

Except for his fussiness at bedtime and the temper tantrums he threw in the small bedroom adjacent to the kitchen in their tiny apartment, Blanche describes Thomas as a good baby, too cute for words, and in some instances describes Thomas's behavior without comment. Where Blanche records an event without comment, it is assumed that the occasion was viewed as normal and acceptable by Thomas's parents. This stands to reason because if something had concerned Blanche, she would have commented on the concern, as she had with other similar observations and comments.

On April 28, 1940, when Thomas was six months, nineteen days old, Blanche's entry indicated that "tantrums" were common occurring events. Events indicate that Blanche was a rather rigid and high-strung person who could not tolerate Thomas's "tantrums." So when Thomas went into one of his "tantrums," Blanche probably remedied the situation by leaving Thomas alone to cry things out and calm down. But were these outbursts of Thomas's really tantrums? Questions about what was causing Thomas's "tantrums" were never addressed in *Our Baby Book*. Was the child hungry? Was the infant experiencing intestinal discomfort? Did the child feel insecure because he did not physically see his mother or father? Was the baby reacting to detergents? Was the infant sensitive to heat? Was the baby ready for a diaper change? The record on these issues is silent. As an adult, Dr. Greenstone acknowledges that in his twenties and thirties he would become annoyed with the prolonged crying of his infant children. The crying of other children did not evoke the same anxious feelings because he did not feel responsible for other children. But, he remembers not being able to quiet his own children and, on occasion, becoming angry with them because they would not "mind" him—an expectation that a 4-month old baby didn't mind him? Could these feelings of frustration have stemmed from the treatment he received as an infant? Was he repeating behaviors his mother exhibited, when she was frustrated and angry with him? The answers to these questions would be no more than educated guesses, as Greenstone's preverbal memories cannot be cognitively resurrected easily, if at all—but it sure looks like a fit.

Blanche noted Thomas smiled and laughed a lot, that teething was no problem, potty training went well, and that Thomas easily adapted to riding in the car. She also noted that eating new foods, reacting to new experiences, changing from a bottle to a glass, from being bathed in a sink to a tub, and changing from a bassinet to a crib were not problems. Blanche observed Thomas's joy of discovery and independence in learning how to walk, drink orange juice, and attempts to verbally communicate with her. Her major concerns revolved around Thomas's health. As Thomas was a couple of week's premature and underweight at birth, Blanche expressly worried when Thomas had a cold or a cough that could turn into pneumonia or whooping cough. Blanche knew that these chronic illnesses were real threats to infants. Also, Thomas was allergic to sulfa drugs, which was the leading treatment against such diseases. This was the time before the advent of antibiotic medicines like penicillin, and baby mortality was high.

During Thomas's first twelve months of life, Blanche would have surely placed Thomas in the "Easy Child" temperamental cluster. He was a joy to his parents as Blanche's final comments show. "Very good so far. Thomas never had any trouble teething. Thomas is a year old and has six teeth, four uppers and two lowers." (10/40)

Blanche saw the first months as going well. She was a proud Mama and loved Thomas dearly. Such was Thomas's introduction into the brave new world, as recorded by Blanche—the dominant figure in Thomas's young life. So, what would Chess and Thomas's take be on Thomas's temperamental constellation placement?

Infant Chart: Thomas's Temperamental Constellation

<u>Temperamental Characteristics</u>	<u>Ratings with Supporting Information</u>
1 Rhythmicity (predictability)	REGULAR: feeding, potty patterns established, but fussy at bed time
2 Approach/ Withdrawal Response	APPROACH: smiles, laughs w/new people, no fuss swallowing cereal, eating meat, sees another baby, person or toy
3 Adaptability (new stimuli)	ADAPTIVE: changes from bassinet to bed, drinks from bottle then to a glass, loves the outdoors, and car rides.
4 Quality Of Mood (amount of pleasant/unpleasant behaviors	VARIABLE: Pleasant behaviors gush when meeting people, playing, exploring, eating, and talking with people. Unpleasant crying, screaming when left alone or doesn't get what he wants.
5 Activity Level (wiggle factor)	HIGH: scoots, climbs up play pen, reaches car bumpers to stand up
6. Threshold Of Responsiveness (evoke response)	VARIABLE: Curious about everything that passes through his field or vision or range of sound, unless engrossed in an activity
7 Intensity Of Reaction (energy level)	HIGH: Positive energy when engrossed in something; intense emotional outbursts when left alone or frustrated.
8 Environmental Distraction Level	NO: Background noise does not distract when baby is engrossed in an activity.
9a Persistence (continuation)	YES: Continues eating bitter spinach even though he's making faces, works hard to turn over, climb to a standing position.
9b Attention Span (length of time)	YES: Engrossed for long periods of time and easily occupies self.

Analysis

Thomas's temperamental profile can be described as regular with regard to biological functions (e.g. eating, potty), but fussy around sleeping times. Generally a happy baby, he exhibits positive approach responses to new events and situations, easily adapts to new stimuli. Thomas also is a highly active baby, showing the persistence necessary to the accomplishment of his objectives coupled with a long attention span. He is responsive to anything within his sight, touch, or sound, but is not distracted by extraneous environmental stimuli. At times, Thomas demonstrates a range of intense frustration behaviors (kicking, crying and screaming until he was blue in the face, and lost his breath.) when his efforts were interrupted, frustrated, or when his objectives were not accomplished.

Thomas's temperament profile does not squarely match any of the Chess and Thomas "Easy Child", "Difficult Child", or "Slow-To-Warm-Up Child" temperament cluster profiles. Thomas probably falls into a profile category of his own. According to Thomas and Chess, thirty-five percent of the research group studied did not match up with the three dominant cluster profiles described. Also, individuals varied within the three dominant temperamental cluster.[9] Rather, Thomas seemed to be part "Easy Child", part "Difficult Child", and part other.

Examining the nature of Blanche's comments about Thomas places her comments into three categories. <u>Purely Objective Comments</u>: "Thomas had his first cold." (12/31/39) "Today Thomas ate cereal for the first time He made faces, but ate it anyway." (2/2/40) "Thomas stands unassisted." (7/31/40) <u>Objective with Neutral or Non-evaluative Comments</u>: "Thomas discovers own hand and feet. They were sure a mystery to him." (1/6/40) "Noticed Thomas creeping on. But we don't allow him to creep much on account of the locality." (7/15/40) <u>Subjective Comments with Biased, Judgmental, and/or Projective Overtones</u>: "Baby Thomas really took a good look at another baby, Francis Beetem, 15 months old—*flirting kind of young—eh?* (1/20/40) "Thomas *holds a glass beautifully*, just as though he had been drinking from one all of his life." (6/24/40) "Thomas has 10 teeth. He has been *a perfect baby in cutting teeth,* no trouble at all." (10/40) Over time it is Blanche's subjective comments with bias, judgmental and/or projective overtones that defines the mother-son relationship—comments that tell Thomas who and what he is in the sight of this powerful Mother, who brought him into the world.

Blanche's purely objective and objective with neutral or non-evaluative comments resemble Chess and Thomas's observations and comments because such are based on facts that are verifiable by any observer. However, none of Chess and

Thomas's comments were made in the presence of the child, and therefore, had no direct affect on the child's self-worth, behavior, and personality development. Chess and Thomas work was based on observing large and varied groups of infants and children,[11] whereas Blanche's work was based on the behaviors of an individual child. Another significant difference is that Chess and Thomas's opinions and judgments are kept out of their data analysis, whereas Blanche's opinions and judgments interact with the data. Blanche's Subjective Judgmental and/ or Projective Comments reflect her values and expectations for Thomas. How well, then, did Thomas measure up to Blanche's standards? Shortly before Thomas's first birthday, Blanche summed up his progress as "Very good so far." (10/ 40) Thomas received mother's conditional "B+" rating for his first twelve months of life. Blanche, like Chess and Thomas, was paying close attention to the child and was gaining important information to positively affect the child's development—but, Blanche's personal self-worth was entangled with the grades she gave Thomas, while the scientists' grading was dispassionate.

Similarly, a description of the father-son relationship can be established based on Sam's grading of Thomas. The important sources of information that shed light on the development and nature of the father-son relationship will be documented and discussed later, however. At this point it is apparent that Sam viewed his son's growth and development as outstanding. Like Blanche, Sam was well pleased with Thomas's progress.

One Year Old

"Today darling is one year old, and we are so thankful for
such a good and healthy baby" (October 9, 1940)

How parents react to their child's behaviors initiates and establishes the quality of parent-child communication, which will be difficult to change as time goes by. During the first year of Thomas's life, Blanche and Sam reacted to Thomas's behaviors in very positive ways. They smiled, exuded pride, spoke in pleasantly toned words, and laughed. When Thomas made a mess while handling a glass of milk or threw his toys from one room to another, Blanche and Sam seemed to understand the behaviors and appeared to understanding and matter of fact in these situations. When the parents consistently read their child's behaviors as an expression of individuality, accept the child's developmental behaviors, and use the information provided by their child's behaviors to learn from and to teach the child in a constructive fashion, the parents are on the right track. Where parents react to their child's behavior in a negative ways, reacting in judgmental, critical, or harsh fashions, the parents have embarked on a negative track, which will, in all probability, not change and become more negative, as the child moves into adolescence. Clearly, the atmosphere in the Greenstone Family Constellation was positive during the first twelve months of Thomas's life.

Chess and Thomas contend that as a child matures, it becomes increasingly more difficult to delineate his temperamental individuality. The problem comes about because other "major categories of behavior, abilities and talents…and motives and goals" are beginning to kick-in at various levels of development and are difficult to distinguish from temperament behaviors.[12]

During the second year of Thomas's life, Blanche's observations and comments, in Thomas's baby book, begin to reflect other behaviors mixed in with temperamental traits. Mingled in with his temperamental traits were social behaviors, such as satisfying the need to be included in a group (bridge game), helping mother clean up the house (picking up clothes and ashtrays), and seeking friends to play with (Danny Cameron, Cousin Steve). With Thomas's ability to crawl and walk, he was becoming more motivated to explore and learn, thereby becoming more independent, meeting more people, doing more things, which further shape and develop his personality.

Developmental and Other Forces

Activity Level: toddling (11/3/40), walks all over the place (11/9/40), picks himself up w/o assistance (1/6/41); wrestles Charlene (1/6/41), Thomas has to be put on a harness (1/1/41), pulls Danny Cameron around in a wagon (1/11/41), throws slipper, toys, etc. out the window (1/28/41), fell off chair (3/3/41), can really do the hula (4/8/41), strips himself of clothing and throws them out the window (4/14/41), throws toys from bedroom into the kitchen (4/15/41)

Exploring: discovers he can do things and gets a bang out of it (1/7/41), ate soap (1/24/41), loves to walk in the Seiren snow (6/1/41)

Approach-Withdrawal: cried through his first hair cut (1/17/41), cried because of carnival noise (4/6/41), food he doesn't like is thrown all over the place (9/16/41)

Social Behaviors: wanted to be included at the bridge table (1/23/41), loves to play with cousin Steve (4/18/41), picks up white clothes and puts them in dirty clothes container (3/10/41), empties ash trays and puts them back in place (6/10/41)

Toilet Training: have been training Thomas for a week (1/28/41), completely broke of wetting (4/4/41, 4/15/41)
Biting: sneaks up and bites people (1/28/41), biting continues (4/15/41)

Personality: he certainly has a good time in his own little world (1/6/41), has a very striking personality (3/3/41)

Independent: Thomas has to be put on a harness or he'll run off (1/1/41), Thomas ate his own supper (3/10/41)

Talking: says first three words in a row (6/17/41)

As Thomas matures, we can still see his temperamental rooted behaviors, shining through the mix of social, personal, and explorative behaviors at the end of his first year.

Thomas's Temperamental Profile

	Temperamental Characteristics	Ratings with Supporting Information
1	Rhythmicity (predictability)	REGULAR: Thomas eats on time and is feeding himself. He is potty trained; plays, sleeps, walks easily and predictably.
2	Approach/ Withdrawal Response	VARIABLE: Positive "striking personality" exploring everything and everyone. Cries at loud unfamiliar noises (haircut, carnival). Throws food around and tips over dishes of foods he doesn't like.
3	Adaptability (new stimuli)	ADAPTIVE: Wrestles back with Charlene. Cooled off at carnival to win a panda bear. Explores everything.
4	Quality Of Mood (amount of pleasant/unpleasant behavior)	VARIABLE: Pleasant behaviors gush when meeting people, playing, exploring, eating, and talking with people. Unpleasant crying, screaming when left alone or doesn't get what he wants.
5	Activity Level (wiggle factor)	HIGH: Discovers he can do things and gets a bang out of it; He's so active; has to be put on a harness I'm afraid he'll run off and hurt himself; eats soap; almost everyone who sees him says Thomas will be a football player; wrestles with Charlene.

6.	Threshold Of Responsiveness (evoke response)	VARIABLE: On one hand he is oblivious to efforts to distract him from his little world. On the other hand, loud noises (electric clippers, loud carnival) evoke crying.
7	Intensity Of Reaction (energy level)	HIGH: Thomas is a spark plug; has a "striking personality". He responds energetically to everyone and everything.
8	Environmental Distraction Level	NO: All extraneous environmental stimuli, including mother's screams, are blocked out.
9a	Persistence (continuation)	YES: Will sneak up and pretend to kiss you, then bites you, despite being swatted.
9b	Attention Span (length of time)	YES: Thomas spends long periods of time involved in exploring and lost within his "own little world."

Analysis

For the first two years of life Thomas seems to behave in predictable ways, given the nine categories of temperament identified in the New York Longitudinal Study (NYLS) conducted by Thomas and Chess. Based on this information Blanche and Sam have sufficient knowledge about Thomas behavior and can easily predict his actions in given situations. As an example, if you were Thomas's parent would you expect him to stand quietly by your side, while you talked to a friend? (Activity level) Would you expect Thomas to enjoy dinner before going to bed? (Rhythmicity) If you took him on a roller-coaster ride for the first time, would he do it? (Approach/withdrawal) If you told him to ask a stranger the time of day, would he do so? (Adaptability) If you called to him to come back to you, would he do so? (Threshold of responsiveness) If you pinched him for doing something wrong, how would he react? (Intensity of reaction) Could you expect Thomas to enjoy each new day? (Quality of mood) Would you expect Thomas to hear the on coming train? (Distractibility) Would you expect Thomas not to play with the dog, after he was told not to play with the dog? (Persistence) If you left Thomas alone, would he be tugging at you ten minutes later? (Attention span) Clearly, these are not difficult questions to answer for parents who have observed and experienced their child's behaviors for a year. Armed with this knowledge a parent would know better than to place their child in the positions posed in the questions and would, thereby, avoid problems before they started. Parents who are aware of their child's temperament and who are willing and able to positively put to use such information will make life more enjoyable and beneficial for their child, as well as themselves.

But, Blanche wasn't prepared for the "train wreck" that was about to happen, when she first perceived that her son had skipped off of the "right track". From Blanche's perspective, something went wrong in April of Thomas's second year of life. Indeed, a look at Blanche's observations and comments show before and after portraits two different sides of Thomas—portraits that baffled Blanche.

Before March 3, 1941 (16 months, 22 days)

"Thomas at this time is the picture of health, as so many strangers remark about it. Certainly makes me happy, because I certainly do everything I can to make this so, and we're so proud of him." (1/6/41)

"A stranger predicted Thomas would be a Criminal Lawyer or an Ambassador…Hot dog! Only time will tells" (1/6/41)

"…never thought one could get so much pleasure from a baby." (1/7/41)

"…we couldn't ask for anything more. He's a very good baby…and has a striking personality, which we hope he will always keep…: (3/3/41)

After April 14, 1941 (18 months, 5 days)

"[Thomas] is getting to be a problem child." (4/14/41)

"Nearly every one who sees Thomas predicts he'll be a football player. He certainly is a mischievous rascal and keeps us on our toes." (6/17/41)

"We are having a time with him…if it is something he doesn't care about, he just throws it all over the place or just tips his mush right over on the table." (9/16/41)

Blanche's writings reveal new words and phrases: "problem child", "mischievous rascal", "keeps us on our toes", and "having a time with him". These comments were not prominent in Blanche's earlier observations and comments recorded in Thomas's baby book.

The first indicator that there was a change in the wind came about as Thomas reached his thirteenth month. Blanche observes and notes Thomas's biting behaviors, but dismisses Thomas's the behaviors, as being just that of a "rascal". (1/28/41)

"Thomas gets a big satisfaction out of biting for some reason, and he is tricky. He comes up to you and makes off he is going to hug and kiss you, and then he does his dirty work. If he sees he is going to get swatted, he just changes his teeth and hugs and kisses you for all he is worth, and then he tries to bite you again, when one is off guard. What a rascal."

At this point several questions come to mind. What was Thomas's reaction to being "swatted" by his mother? What did Blanche know about temperament development and child development? What was Blanche thinking as her child began to assert himself and/or act out?

Swatting Thomas

How hard were these "swats"? How long has "swatting" been used to correct Thomas's behaviors? In practice "swatting" probably ranged from a playful love-tap to a quick, sharp blow administered to stop the repeated behavior once and for all. As for how long had "swatting" been used to set limits to Thomas's behaviors, the answer is probably all along. And, what was Thomas's response after being swatted? He comes right back to bite again. (Persistence) This time he feigns a kiss and a hug before biting. Thus, another classic issue raises its head: Is there a legitimate role for corporal punishment when raising children? As with so many questions dogging child-raising practices, the answer is, it depends. The bias of this author is corporal punishment has no place in any child raising process. Parents are all-powerful and omnipotent in the eyes of their children and have a host of nonviolent means to teach or discipline their children.

Blanche Just Didn't Know Any Better and Sam Was Out of the Loop.

Blanche was certainly a willing parent who wanted to do the best she could for her child in whom she took great pride and Blanche was a highly capable individual. But timing was not in her favor. There was a lot that Blanche didn't know, which could have helped her avoid the "perceived" train wreck. The Thomas and Chess research wasn't conceived until the early 1950's.[13] The study wasn't completed and published for professional use (e.g., counselors, psychologists, and social workers) until the early 1970's, and didn't catch the public eye until the 1980's. By the early 80's Thomas was in his 40's and his children were 14 and 16 years of age! Oops, a little late for Kim and Michael. But granddaughter, Megan, is four months old today, so the timing factor is as perfect for eliminating negative family traits, as it has been in the past three generations! [jj]

During Blanche's childhood spare-the-rod-and-spoil-the-child was the dominant child raising philosophy. As a parent, Blanche was well aware that "environmental determinism" was the way to raise children. The scientific literature of her day (1920's–1950's) said that the decisive factor in shaping human growth and development was the environment within which a child was raised—the better the environment, the better the child.[14] Further, in Blanche's day the mother was held solely responsible for ensuring that the child was raised properly in the family environment, which was supported by the income provided by the father. For that matter, medical information about the deleterious affects that smoking, drinking alcohol, and the use of other drugs have on the developing fetus, on the quality of breast milk, and on parenting practices was yet to come. Also, the educational level of the mother and the psychological and emotional wellness of the mother are key factors associated with healthy family environments. Blanche did not finish high school and Blanche had issues. Of course the father is not exempt from the responsibility of knowing what healthy practices need to be practiced. But like Blanche, most fathers and mothers just didn't know all those facts or think about how their actions affected their children in the 1930's. Their lament was, "Every day in every way I'm doing the best that I can for this child." But, what happens if the parent's best is flawed?

While the parent's lament contains truth, the lament masks a multitude of family behaviors and patterns, which are passed on to their children, who pass variations or reversals of these behaviors and patterns onto their children. Family behaviors and patterns, which are cyclically passed on from generation to generation are sometimes good (moral values and the value of continuing education), sometimes bad (traditions of alcoholism and patterns of criticism and fault finding), and sometimes ugly (parental raging and family incest). These cycles of good, bad, and ugly need to be identified and understood by fathers and mothers, grandparents, great-grandparents, etc., and need to be sustained in the family order, if good, and eliminated from the family order, if bad or ugly. Raising children is not a short race; it's a marathon—a marathon that runs continually from generation to generation. The family reward for running a good marathon is that the family usually continues and prospers. The family reward for running a bad or ugly marathon is that the family is destroyed and, in time, extinguished.

What Was Blanche Thinking?

As was discussed before, Blanche's baby book comments about Thomas fall into three categories: purely objective, objective with neutral or non-evaluative comments, and subjective with overtones of bias, value judgments and/or projection.

It's the latter category that will be examined next, as that is where Blanche revealed her hidden motivators, which subconsciously drove her, as she raised her only child.

At least four interpersonal dynamics seem to be at play within Blanche. First, "I" derive happiness and pleasure from having such a wonderful, interesting baby. Second, "I" do my best to make sure the baby is a good baby. Third, "I" hope things remain perfect. Fourth, even strangers validate "my" work. Certainly, there is no problem with a mother's pride in her child. But, there is a danger where the mother does not individuate from her child. From Blanche's perspective it appears that she and Thomas are same individual. Whose psychological-emotional needs are being met when the strangers complement Blanche on Thomas's health, striking personality, and potential to become an ambassador or lawyer? Blanche really believes that Thomas and her destinies are tied together. That could spell problems between mother and son down the line. What happens, if Blanche's good baby appears to others as going bad? The question posed can be generalized: What happens when any good baby appears to turn bad? By now, this line of questions should make most readers cringe, as if hearing someone just scraped their fingernails across a chalkboard. Blanche appears to take things personally and appears to view the outside world, and her world in black and white terms.

Will this mother take responsibility for a "bad" baby? The answer is absolutely not. Thomas's persistence, his dominant temperamental characteristic bestowed by nature, becomes the bane of his mother's existence. Blanche does not understand that the temperamental traits of children are, *per se,* never the root of deviant behavior.[15] But this exactly how Blanche views her son. And, it is this misalignment in Blanche's perception that strikes a discordant timbre within the Greenstone Family, the first and foremost of society's institutions.

The Second Piece:
Matures Through Biologically Driven
Developmental Stages

Before we move too much further with Blanche, Thomas, and Sam (Who?), it's important that we touch on several of the contributions child growth and development research offer to us and that we attempt to compare Thomas's behaviors with those of other children his own age.

Let's see do we start with the Piagetian school of thought, Gesellian thought, or Dr. Phil? Oh, ennie-meanie-minie-mo let's take a look at Rudolf Dreikurs, *Children: The Challenge.*[16] Dreikurs was a child psychologist practicing in Chicago. His premise was that human behavior is purposeful and goal oriented. Humans are social beings and need to feel that they have a place in a group, be it family, friends, colleagues, society. In line with this, Dreikurs believes that attention-getting behaviors, power struggles, retaliatory behaviors, and behaviors showing lack of confidence result from misunderstandings or uncertainties a child has about events happening in his immediate environment (i.e. family). Rewards and punishments do not have any place in the home or school environments. Instead, Dreikurs suggests the use of natural and logical consequences, when dealing with children who bounce across reasonable boundaries set by parents.

When Thomas bites Blanche, should Blanche bite him back or swat him? Blanche should do neither. Rather, Blanche should calmly enter into polite and respectful conversation with Thomas about biting hurts. If the biting persists mother needs to hold Thomas to the logical or natural consequences of his inability to control his biting. Mother may tell Thomas that because Thomas can't be trusted not to bite, Thomas and mother can't go see Mickey Mouse at the Fox Oakland Theater[ff] this afternoon because Thomas might bite someone and cause him or her pain. This discussion needs to happen without screaming and yelling on mother's part. And the conversation should certainly not be delivered in the heat of anger, but when both mother and son are at peace. As Thomas's reaction, considering his high intensity of response and persistence, will probably be immediate, negative, and explosive, the time and place for the conversation needs to be carefully planned—say 9:00 A.M. in a park with a large grassy open field. Hint: After mother calmly drops the bomb on junior about no movie as the consequence of his biting behavior, that's the end of conversation on that subject from mother no matter how many "mommy pleases" or "I'm going to eat worms and die..." statements junior makes. Junior is left to feel the consequences of his own actions. Tomorrow is another day. But today, the consequence is irrevocable. Dreikurs' books are a worthwhile read for parents.

Several other developmentalists work is also well worth a parents' time to study. Frances Ilge, Louise Bates Ames, and Sidney Baker have built on the research of Dr. Arnold Gesell, a pediatric psychologist who founded the Yale Clinic for Child Development in 1911. Two central ideas that Gesell formed were: 1. As children pass through stages of development, they also exhibit times of *equilibrium* and *disequilibrium*—periods when they seem to "click" and periods when they seem to "forget" it all. His rationale was as children enter a new stage of growth and development, previously learned skills are placed on the back burner. 2. Gesell believed that a person's body type (i.e., Ectomorph, Mesomorph, and Endomoph) limits what a person can do. While I can't fully buy some of Gesell's ideas, such as body types limiting or almost determining one's behavior, I do consider his skillful research and display of children's behavior in chronological order to have been an immense contribution to ordinary people, as well as to the field of psychology.[17]

As we followed Chess and Thomas's temperamental development from birth to twenty-four months, we will now follow Gesell's ages and stages of motor and social development for children at sixteen weeks of age, fifty-two weeks of age, and for eighteen months of age.[18] Clearly, when a parent has some idea of that to expect, their shock and upset are mollified, when their little darling turns into a "little monster."

By 16 Weeks Of Age

<u>Motor Behavior</u>: Feeding goes better. Sleeps more easily—even through the night. Attains "swimming position" when on stomach with arms and legs stretched out with abdomen well up off the floor. Eyes follow a moving object. Arms reach, but no grasping, yet.

<u>Social Behavior</u>: Likes being on a big bed; and likes to be held or propped up so he can face the world eyes front—baby's eyes glisten and face breaks out into a smile when lifted. Baby coos, chuckles, and laughs aloud.

Thomas really smiled for the first time. (10/16/39) Baby really noticed for the first time a toy hanging from his bassinet. (10/29/39) First time baby smiled a lot and wanted to play nearly all day. Laughed out loud: 9 weeks old. (12/12/39) Baby played with rattle, 9 weeks and 3 days old and discovered me for the first time. (12/14/39) Tried to roll from side to side also tried to talk! (12/19/39) Baby carried on quite a conversation of goo's etc. Sure is cute. (12/26/39) Thomas discovers own hand and feet. They were sure a mystery to him. (1/6/40) Thomas took a nap for the first time sleeping on his back. Up until this time, he has always slept on his stomach. (1/17/40) Baby Thomas really took a good look at another baby.... (1/20/40) Today Thomas ate cereal for the first time. He made faces, but ate it anyway. (2/2/40) He recognized Teddy Bear and played with it. Sure is cute. (2/4/40) Thomas knows how to shake hands. (2/840) Today, Thomas is 4 months old and ate all his cereal (1-teaspoon) without making any fuss. (2/9/40)

By Fifty-Two Weeks of Age

Motor Behavior: The baby creeps around freely on hand s and knees and can take a few steps with hands holding onto furniture. May want to stand when fed and manipulate spoon himself.

Social Behavior: Serene, confident, and friendly, the baby loves an audience, recognizes social approval, and repeats performances laughed at. Baby enjoys the give and take of social games (peek-a-boo) and loves to be chased.

Note: Increased motor abilities may interfere with daily routines, but give the baby the scope to use his newfound abilities.

At 7 months Thomas loves to tear up paper. (3/4/40) Thomas used the potty for the first time. (3/27/40) Thomas held a glass of water and drank it. He spilled water all over the place, and he sure was cute. (4/4/40) Thomas held his baby bottle by himself. (5/13/40) Thomas shakes his head back and forth when we say no! No! Too cute for words. (6/40) Thomas stood up by himself with the aid of his playpen (8 months, 1 day old). He tries so hard to talk more so than walking. (6/10/40) Thomas holds a glass beautifully, just as though he had been drink from one all his life. (6/24/40) Noticed Thomas creeping on. But we don't allow him to creep much on account of the locality. (7/15/40) At 9 and 1/2 months with our aid Thomas would take a step or two. (7/16/40) And now he gets around his playpen at 9 and 1/2. (7/26/40) Dr. Torrano dropped in to see the baby when all of a sudden baby waived good-bye. (7/2540) Thomas stands unassisted. (7/31/40) Thomas climbs up his playpen and reaches for things like car bumpers, steps, car running boards to hold onto while he stands up. (9/12/40)

By Eighteen Months

Behavior: The dart, dash, and fling age as the baby moves through the fifteen months stage onto a one-way street where the baby moves in the opposite direction than the adult has in mind. And he/she seldom obeys verbal commands and cannot stand to be frustrated—quick temper and needs everything now.

Social Behavior: His mind is dominated by the idea of taking and not giving. Often treats other children as if they were objects—stepping on them rather than walk around. No idea of sharing.

Motor Behavior: Unsteady: can walk, run, climb, but his balance is very shaky. He understands more words than he can say, but his understanding is very limited.

Note: If you expect very little, keep your demands that he "mind" to a minimum, and give very close and rather constant physical supervision, you may find that you will get on well with and enjoy your 18-monther (not monster).

Thomas at 1 and 1/2 years old is getting to be a problem child. In a cute way he strips himself of all clothing and throws everything out the window. (4/14/41) When he kisses you on his own accord, you can rest assure he is going to get into mischief. Thomas still has the bad habit of biting people. (4/15/41) Nearly everyone who sees Thomas predicts he'll be a football player. He certainly is a mischievous rascal and keeps us on our toes. (6/17/41)Blanche and Sam seem to have taken the eighteen month stage behaviors in stride, but Ilg, Ames, and Baker developmental stages foretell of both rolling calms and furious stormy seas ahead—an emotional roller coaster, which fits Thomas almost to a "T".[19]

- Two-year old: Baby is more developmentally organized and demonstrates steady improvement.

- Two-and-a-Half Years: This is an age about which parents may need warning because so much that the child now does naturally, almost inevitably, is directly contrary to what his parents would like.

- Three-year Old: Things quiet down, briefly, at three for most children. The three-year old seems to love to conform.

- Three-and-a-Half: Temporarily at three many children reach what most parents and teachers consider a delightful stage of equilibrium.

- Four-year Old: Out of Bounds and Out of Your Control—loud silly laughter, fits of rage, kicking, hitting, throwing stones, imagination without reason, and the language guaranteed to shock anyone, except a wise and hardened nursery-school teacher!

Thomas and Chess's work on temperament and the research of Gesell, Ilge, Ames, and Baker on ages and stages show parents and society the basic genetic hand dealt to their fledgling member of society and how to play that hand through the child's early development.[20] The next ingredient, which is continually folded into Thomas's personality[21] from conception through adulthood,[22] is the social interaction that takes place within Thomas's triadic family constellation: Blanche, Sam, and Thomas.

Two Years Old

Given our previous discussions, one shouldn't be shocked by the news that temperament and passage through various stages of development do not create abnormal behavior.[15] However, consonance and dissonance between an infant and its environment (i.e., family, school, church, and society) does contribute greatly to the degree of internal turmoil and/or overt deviant behavior exhibited by a child. The relationship between a child and society affect and shape the attitudes of both; and such relationships, by their natures, produce a blend of accord and friction. The relations between the child and society begin within the family institution, in this case, the triadic family constellation of Blanche, Sam, and Thomas. In this family constellation the mother is the sun, moon, and stars within Thomas's child's eyes. The most prevailing force shaping a baby's development is the mother's attitude toward and communication with her child.

Study the interactions between mother and child. What is your take on the degree of positive attitudes and quality communication established by Blanche and Thomas's interactions? Where is there accord? Where is their friction? And, how smooth is their blending?

Third Year Mother And Son Interactions

Dates	Events	Interactions
10/9/41	>Went shopping	>Had a grand day.
10/9/41	>Nap then pictures	>Thomas played with Danny
10/9/41	>Halloween dinner	>Thomas didn't know what to make of his birthday cake.
10/10/41	>Thomas plays on roof and falls skinning his knee.	>Blanche tries to help, but Thomas wants to take care of himself. Blanche feels he is too independent.
10/29/41	>Thomas talks and yells at theater.	>Blanche took Thomas out of the theater and he started crying
10/29/41	>Thomas nibbles on butter cubes	>Blanche sees teeth marks on every butter cube placed on the table.

10/29/41	>Hears song and repeats words	>Blanche impressed with Thomas's ability at two years old.
10/29/41	>Mother "gets after" Thomas.	>Thomas displays temper; Blanche comments about Thomas "telling me plenty".
10/18/41	>Thomas talks to everyone.	>Blanche seems to delight in son's behavior and records events.
2/42	>Thomas repeats everything	>Blanche records this fact.
2/25/42	>Thomas and Mom love Robert, Mary's 1 year old.	>Blanche observes Thomas loves to play with Robert; and thinks they will be good friends.
3/42	>Thomas wets bed once a week.	>Blanche thinks that's pretty good for a boy his age, so they say. Also, Thomas is a "perfect roughneck."
3/42	>Pulled teapot on head. He's into everything.	>We're just about to put in reform school, God bless him...
3/10/42	>Thomas pores pee into bathtub	>Sam was taking a bath at the time; Blanche just recorded the fact.
3/21/42	>Thomas's first over night stay	>Blanche cries all night and Sam is sad as Thomas is away from home.
4/18/42	>Thomas has a girl friend, Patty.	>Mother allows Patty and Thomas to go everywhere with each other.
7/42	>Thomas says, "Go easy," when his face is washed.	>Blanche records event.
7/42	>Recites, "Three Little Pigs".	>Blanche records event.
8/42	> Says his prayers all by himself.	>Blanche records event.

Analysis
Mother (Age 33) and Son (Age 2)

At some level the mother-son interactions, according to Blanche's records, are going swimmingly. Thomas is a character, who gets into a lot of mischief, but who is loved and valued by his parents, including Sam! Thomas is socially outgoing, talks to everyone he meets, and has a pal up in the mountains, Patty. Blanche is impressed and proud of Thomas's development and notes Thomas's annoying biting behaviors and temper when she "gets after" him. "So far so good," but Blanche's record is half the story.

Thomas's backward view to this time is different in that the particulars of Blanche's disciplinary interventions are more pronounced.[25] Dr. Greenstone recalls that his behaviors are met with immediate and forceful reactions: yelling, grabbing, being dragged into the closet, door slamming, swats, slaps, hitting with coat hangers and slippers. Thomas's immediate behavioral responses are to recover from the pain (spanking, slapping) or adapt to the punishment situation (closet) or to rage back at Blanche. But, after recovery, he would be back at it, with the same punishing results.

From Blanche's perspective the blending of accord and friction in their relationship is reasonably balanced. From Thomas's perspective, because his sun, moon, and stars are falling in on him, he enjoys the accord and he bounces back from the punishments, but the friction is accumulating.

Father (age 31) and Son (age 2)

Blanche penned two incidents, which present us with a glimpse of Sam's interactions with his son. The pee dumping on Sam event seemed to be recorded as a humorous happening. There is no record of Thomas being punished for pouring pee on his dad. The fact that Sam was "blue" when Thomas stayed overnight at his sister's house indicates a loving, affectionate bond existed between father and son. In point of fact, almost every family picture with Thomas and Sam in it shows Sam to be genuinely delighted to be with his son.[bb] There were differences in temperament and personality between Blanche and Sam—opposites had attracted each other in marriage. It was Sam's nature not to react to the small stuff. Blanche, on the other hand, felt everything was important. At this point in time Thomas was alone with Blanche twelve hours a day and was with Sam and Blanche four hours a day. What would happen, if the percentages were reversed? How would Thomas's life be shaped, if the percentages of time with each parent were reversed? This is obviously a question, which can only be answered theoretically, as fate/God did not allow that road to be taken..

Blanche leaves us with the general impression that Sam was a good provider and father, quiet figure in the family's background, as if he were almost a ghostly presence.

The Third Piece:
Raised as Their Parents Were Raised

As child raising practices were discussed in some detail in Part I, we will only briefly handle the subject at this point.

In 1939 the proper way to raise a child was about the same as it had been in the 1880's. Spare the rod and spoil the child. Society encouraged parents to keep their children in strict account and to use physical punishment liberally. Exclusively, Blanche bore the responsibility for creating a nurturing home environment and for the proper upbringing of Thomas in that environment, as was the mode of her times. She closely monitored his health and made sure he received the best medical attention possible. She was responsible for Thomas's behavior.

Sam's role was to provide for the family, which he did well, and handle Thomas when Blanche was frustrated. This took two forms. When Blanche told Sam it's time for Thomas to get a good belting, Sam usually carried out Blanche's wishes. However, left to his own devices, Sam was not a "spare the rod and spoil the child" type. His disciplinary approach was more of a "open the child's mind and let him reflect" type. And, he distanced himself from the battles that Blanche and Thomas would mount on each other.

The idea that the wife was a less understanding person and more of a harsh disciplinarian than her husband ran contrary to what one would expect within a family in the 1930's and 1940's. But, in this case, Blanche was the Dominant star, whose brilliance filled the home and obliterated lesser stars.

The Fourth Piece:
Learns by Experience

Described by Blanche as a "perfect roughneck"[s] Thomas begins his twenty-fourth month of life by being allowed to play on the mortuary roof when his mother is hanging clothes out to dry. Thomas plays on a gravel rooftop surrounded by a four-foot high brick wall atop the two-story mortuary. Those air vents behind him[v] are from the Greenstone's kitchen and bathroom. There are scores of these sharp edged sheet metal topped vents protruding through the roof from the morgue rooms, the Jew room, casket rooms, chapels, and the Caporgno's apartment—all ready to slice a thigh, an arm, or a back and cut down a spirited two-year old dashing across the roof. Blanche was justifiably afraid that Thomas would hurt himself and took sharp measures to stop him, but Thomas continued to push the envelope and reaped Blanche's wrath. Thomas's persistence was a two-edged sword. Swung one way, Thomas did not seem to learn by experience.

Swung the other way, Thomas accomplished much more than less persistent children could.

Thomas's persistence draws Blanche's praise and criticism, loving and yelling, lecturing and swatting depending on the situation. Then, Blanche is surprised when Thomas displays his temper. At 24 months and 20 days old Thomas angrily strikes back and tells Blanche plenty. Why? My guess is that Thomas was learning how to protect himself from Blanche's harsh discipline, which ironically was intentioned to protect her son from harm. Blanche does not understand the phenomenon that was taking place before her eyes. Angrily "getting after" Thomas terrifies him, as much as Goliath terrified the Israelites!

"As soon as the Israelites saw Goliath, they ran from him and were terrified."
(The Jerusalem Bible: 1ˢᵗ Samuel 17.24)

Blanche at five feet, two inches tall and about one hundred eight pounds compared to Thomas at two feet, six inches and thirty-two pounds was actually of greater proportions than Goliath was to David. Blanche was not from an enemy camp; she was Thomas's mother, his sun, moon, and stars. She was with Thomas day-in-and-day-out. During that time, Thomas couldn't run away; he was totally dependent on his mother for food, freedom to move about, love, and protection. Many parents do not realize the awesome power they have over their children. Blanche is surprised by son's angry outbursts (10/29/41) and guesses that Thomas preverbal angry display has something to do with "getting after for doing something" (10/29/41) She guessed right, but still keeps on whacking him, when she is displeased with his behavior. In time Thomas's anger reactions turn into uncontrollable behaviors (3/41), then his behaviors are viewed as steadily evolving into a pattern of willfully defiance (7/9/43). The irony, of course, is that despite Blanche's opinion that her son was going haywire, Thomas behavior was actually progressing well developmentally. The unintended consequences of Blanche's insisting on consistently correcting her child's misbehaviors by physically restraining and striking the boy, frightened Thomas out of his wits. When pummeled by mother for doing something wrong, Blanche did not fathom that Thomas's "temper" was a primitive fight-flight reflex that she had unwittingly triggered, as she physically and verbally attacked her son.

A faithful dog, when kicked in the flank by a heretofore-loving master, may turn and growl at his master or even bite. When Thomas's loving mother "got after" him, he growled and barked at his mother in self-defense. A mixture of rage and adrenaline fueled primitive language and aggressive behavior was a counter-attack. Blanche doesn't see her hand in this mess, as she was raising Thomas in much the same way that she was raised and in much the same way she raised her younger brothers, Fred and Joe. After all that's how most parents were taught and expected to raise their children from time *ad memoriam*.

> "A father who loves his son will whip him often, so that he can be proud of him later. If a son is disciplined, he will be of some use, and his father can boast of him to his friends. A man who gives good guidance to his son cannot only take pride in him among his friends, but he can make his enemies jealous. While the father is alive, the sight of his son makes him happy. And when he dies, he has no regrets. He is not really dead, because his son is like him. He has left someone to take vengeance on his enemies and to return the favors he owes his friends." (Holy Bible, St. Jerome Edition, Book of Sirach, Chapter 30, Verses 1-6)

This slice of life from 160 B.C. gives us the history behind the "spare the rod and spoil the child" philosophy, which was employed in most households in 1942, the twist being that it's the mother who is chiefly responsible for holding the child to account.

Thomas is loved and valued at times. He is swatted and gotten after at other times. Throughout all this what was Thomas experiencing and learning? He was learning one way to protect himself from the Goliath's of this world. He was learning to fear and hate his mother and anyone else that wore the displeased mask his mother wore, while criticizing, blaming, and/or attacking him.. As an adult, Dr. Greenstone admits that he always had trouble with authority figures, who acted like his mother in distressed times. He was learning that when you do things "bad" you get swatted and when you do things "good" you get patted on the popo. He was learning not to be open and honest in all respects. He was learning to emotionally distance himself from painful situations. He was learning that might makes right. Thomas was learning when mommy smiles, that's good and when mommy frowns that's not good. He was learning to be a perfect little man to please mother. And finally, Thomas learned he was the identified problem in the Greenstone family—a lesson he learned at his mommy's knee.

Didn't Thomas learn anything positive at his mother's knee? Absolutely, Blanche could be a loving, caring, organized, selfless individual who built for Thomas a morale foundation, which told Thomas what was right and what was wrong. Blanche, also, modeled a strong work ethic for Thomas, which eventually facilitated his success in graduate school and his success in the work place. Numerous passages in *Our Baby Book* clearly show the fine contributions Blanche gave to her son: love, care, food, warmth, encouragement, support, and celebrations.

Flawed parenting (nobody's perfect) does not necessarily negatively affect the outcome of children for a variety of reasons. As temperaments differ, some children are easier and more pliable than others. Where children experience harshness from one parent, the other parent may mitigate the negative circumstances. Where parents are unduly harsh, there may be other adults or children that mitigate the negative affects of a parent-child relationship (e.g., grandmas, grandpas, brothers, sisters, friends, aunts, cousins, neighbors, or pastors). Thomas did have people and situations, which did help to balance his young life: Grandma Freitas, Grandpa Joe, Auntie Esther, Charlene, Mary Caporgno, Mrs. Arnold, pets, and his father.

Further, research on the subject of resiliency, as that done by Robert Brooks and Sam Goldstein, support the notion that many children who elude horrendous family hazards have "resilient mind sets", which permit them to cope with and overcome adversity.[23] Brooks and Goldstein worked with hundreds of children whom, despite parental abuse, racism, and other hard knocks of life, have become healthy and functional adults, who live productive lives.

Like is the case in all families, a mixed bag of the good, the bad, and the ugly is handed down from one generation to another. These experiences are the materials from which our lives are, in part, shaped. This is the mixed bag that teaches us a variety of lessons. So it was with Thomas and his family.

Three Years Old

Most parents find the age of three to be a time when "things quiet down". Three years of age is considered by the Gesell people as a "delightful stage of equilibrium".[24]

October 9, 1942 through April 25, 1943

Thomas is stringing words together to make sentences, "Mommy, here me is." "You do dat like me does." He repeats everything you say and sings songs. Thomas delights in running away from Blanche every chance he gets. Loves wrestling matches, talking to strangers, and going over to Scotty's house to bum candy and oranges.

July, 1943 through September 6, 1943

Thomas is pulled out of Sunday School because of his fighting. Blanche is at her "wits end" because Thomas gets up early in the morning and roams around the block only to get hauled back home by neighbors. For running off again, Thomas gets a "terrible licking" with a coat hanger that left him with black and blue marks on his legs. He has the annoying habit of spitting. Thomas has no fear of anything—a daredevil. He loves classical music. An employee at the mortuary slaps Thomas. He's bossy orders people around, demanding and has a ton of girlfriends.

So much for quieting down at age three—individual differences, you know. Thomas's spitting behaviors were the last straw. Maybe it's just a stage he's going through or, as Driekers says, "all behavior is purposeful." What purpose does spitting accomplish? Possibly Thomas is trying to draw more attention to himself? Possibly he's getting even with his mother for her criticisms and physical punishments? Possibly, he's mimicking tobacco chawing President Zachary Taylor or Grandpa Joe spittin' tobacco out on the garage floor in Martinez? Thomas's behavior seems to have jumped ahead into the four-year old stage of development, where behaviors are completely out of bounds. At three and a half years of age Thomas seems to Blanche to be an uncontrollable monster. Blanche is on the ropes and going down for the count. Parenting isn't a pugilistic contest to determine who is the winner. However, Blanche keeps slugging away at Thomas in the same old way; and Thomas keeps reacting in the same old way. One thing for sure, Sam is distancing himself far away from the din and roar of battle.

Analysis

Blanche, aware that she is turning gray before her time, writes an underlined desperate manifesto. Confessing her good intentions as a parent to her three-year old child and the world, Blanche declares, "It's not my fault." "I did the best I can." As was the case when Christ was brought before Pontus Pilot, Blanche has washed her hands clean of the whole mess.

> "Thomas I'm writing all of this down, so that when you have children of your own, you will understand, I hope. (Understand twenty-four years hence what you don't understand now.) No matter how much worry and trouble you have given us (You're the problem.), we wouldn't give you up for all the gold in the world. (But, we still love you.) Only because we love you more than anything else in the world, but you sure are a character (We love you, but make no mistake about it, you caused this mess.) and maybe some day you will be a great person. (Maybe the end result will validate my self-worth and hard work.)"

Blanche has just thrown in the towel on parenthood. Shazam! Blanche is not to be blamed for their three-year old having fallen off the narrow road of righteousness into the pit of darkness—the bad seed incarnate that he is. If there is a reader that finds him/herself nodding in agreement with Blanche, the reader should probably not bring children into his/her life. If the reader is affirmatively nodding at this point and has children, severe damage is being done to your children—get into family therapy, pronto.

Blanche only had two arrows in her quiver for raising children (love them and use the rod when they misbehave). Blanche had loved her baby with all of her heart and the results had gone far beyond her expectations. From ages birth through January 7, 1941 (15 months old), Blanche writes, "…never thought one could get so much pleasure from a baby." Thomas had fulfilled her life. Blanche was riding high on a cloud with a silver lining, until things began to unravel, probably as far back as January 28, 1941, when Thomas was getting swatted for biting. From that point onward we see the silver-lined cloud become tarnished when all attempts to change Thomas's "negative behavior" failed. Then in July of 1943, while deep in the dark caverns of despair, Blanche stumbled on what she believed to be the root cause of Thomas's problems.

> "I believe a lot of Thomas's problems are caused from being tied up, and no back yard to play. When we went to Merced on our vacation, he was no trouble at all. He was so busy playing, because underneath all of his mischief, he is very kind hearted and thoughtful." *(Our Baby Book)*

Blanche's belief was more insightful than she realized. By getting Thomas outside of the house as often as possible, Thomas would be playing (i.e., exploring, learning, developing) guided by natural consequences and his judgment and choices, rather than being beaten like a mule into submission. Blanche's theory about "Thomas's problem" worked, not quite for the reasons she thought, but close enough for practical purposes. Living in a small apartment and having only the small porch two-stories up, outside of the kitchen was not the root cause of "Thomas's problem". The nature of the mother-son relationship was the problem, which Blanche couldn't grasp. Blanche couldn't quite comprehend that Thomas's two and three-year old developmental behaviors were not deliberate. She saw him as a fully in tact, little, but grown person who willfully defied her. With tears of love in her eyes, Blanche would continue to scream and pummel Thomas in an attempt to bring him under control—her crusade lasted longer than the Second World War and the Korean conflicts put together. Separating the two would definitely help ease the tension between the two persistent and dominant children: Blanche, the first born child v. Thomas the only child.

To say that the match between Thomas and his mother left something to be desired is a bit of an understatement. Blanche was a perfectionist. She prides herself, and rightfully so, on her ability to organize and control the outcome of events—a key to her success as the first daughter in the Frietas family, success as the head usherette at the Stage Theater, success at managing her marriage and household, and a success through the first twelve months of motherhood. During the second twelve months of motherhood, the perfect dream-child, in whom Blanche took great pride and delight, began to show signs of unraveling. Now, in his third twelve-month slice of life, Thomas had on his own accord evolved into an unmanageable willful little horror; and Armageddon was at hand. As William Bendix (a comedian Blanche loved) would say, "What a revoltin' development this is!" Except Blanche wasn't laughing as the wheels were falling off her happy wagon. Worse, Blanche perceived Thomas's behavior as a distasteful reflection on her efforts as a mother. She had been stripped of her pride, worth, and success due to this child turning out to be the rotten apple in the barrel.

Four Years Old

Blanche states that she and Sam would like to have a birthday party for Thomas, but the apartment is too small; so parties will have to wait until later, thereby reinforcing the theory that lack of room in the apartment was the cause of Thomas's problems

Thomas continues to misbehave. He interrupts Mrs. Jones, a church leader, before the playing of "Oh, come All Ye Faithful" to instead play "Lay That Pistol Down Babe." Thomas dismantles a pocket watch Sam gave to him, which caused Blanche to hit boiling point and wonders, "I don't know why he breaks everything he puts his hands on?" Thomas knows, "Shut up" is a "bad word" and corrects his mother when Blanche tells him to "Shut up your big mouth." He mooches hamburger from the butcher at Saggs Meat Market. When scolded by Blanche, Thomas repeats her comments. "Why did you do that?" "Why did you do that?" Asked how a hole was cut into his pajamas, Thomas answers, "A moth." Thomas takes ants to bed with him in a bag. And, he tunes into his radio programs each morning all by himself. On September 11, 1944 Thomas enters Kindergarten, four years and eleven months old.

Analysis

Thomas has reached the classic four-year old stage of life—out of bounds in every direction. According to developmentalists a parent will inevitably:

> "...need to use a good deal of firmness in dealing with your 4-year-old. But you will feel less hopeless and less angry if you can keep in mind that behaving in and out-of-bounds manner is not only an almost inevitable but a probably quite necessary part of Four's development."[26]

As was mentioned earlier, Blanche was a mother in the 1930's when such notions were unknown to the general public. The average parent believed that the only remedy that would change a spoiled brat was to obliterate him/her into submission. The little bastard was willfully defying their authority of the parent and must be crushed into obeying.

By four years of age the battle lines between mother and son were firmly drawn and would last nearly to the end of Blanche's lifetime, the affects of which would be felt by Thomas well into his adulthood.

The Fifth Piece:
Shaped By Interactions with Nature

Had there been no intervening, mitigating events, which separated Blanche from Thomas, there is no telling what would have happened to three-year old Thomas, let alone thirty-four year old Blanche. While out-of-doors, on vacations, and playing in the back of the mortuary, Thomas experienced the wonders of nature and learned about nature and natural consequences.

The highest good is like water.
Water gives life to the ten thousand things and does not strive.
It flows in places men reject and so is like the Tao.
In dwelling, be close to the land.
In meditation, go deep in the heart.
In dealing with others, be gentle and kind.
In speech, be true.
In ruling, be just.
In business, be competent.
In action, watch the timing.
No fight: No blame.[27]

With Thomas out doors nature became one of his great teachers. As early as June 1, 1941, when he was one year old, Thomas is introduced to the wonders of the Sierra Mountains in Northern California. His vacations to the mountains continue for several years.[n, t, u, z] In the Sierra's Thomas would sit on a large rock among the cattails and endlessly watch the quiet, dark flow of icy water rush over boulders on its way to the ocean.

> The highest good is like water.
> Water gives life to the ten thousand things and does not strive.
> It flows in places men reject so is like the Tao.

Walking from the stream, up the mountain slope to the cabin, Thomas would reach a spot where the river sounds ceased to be. Sitting on a granite outcrop, the still fragrance of the pine forest overtook his senses and soul.

> In dwelling be close to the land.
> In meditation go deep in the heart.

Soon something would stir on the forest floor or in the tree boughs, or in the air. Thomas would sit contented for a time entertained and fascinated by his surroundings.

> No fight; No blame.

Nature's ways sat in stark contrast to the ways of home and family. At home was turmoil and apprehension. The Mountainous terrain, the trees, and wild life gave Thomas understanding, tranquility, and wonder.

> No fight; No blame.

Each vacation to the mountains, oceans, and farmlands deepened Thomas's love and appreciation of nature. In all ways nature is the perfect teacher. When one is slapped, spanked, or pinched by a parent or teacher, hatred, revenge, and injustice may be felt and directed back at the parent or teacher. When running through a stand of bushes, falling off a bolder, or getting caught by an ocean wave beats one-up, the same emotions do not come into play. The difference? The wilderness teaches by natural consequences, which are consistent, and are not judgmental. In the example given above, humans taught by inflicting consequences, which vary from person to person and from time to time, and are highly judgmental. Nature's laws can be understood and relied upon. Human laws can't be fully understood and relied upon. Because human laws are administered unevenly, they often teach children how play the blame game and not take responsibility for their actions. The blame game doesn't work nature.

Thomas loved nature and sought nature within the pungent gardens in the neighborhood, walks around Lake Merritt, playing in deFermery Park, fishing off the Berkeley Pier, watching cloud formations, standing in the rain and wind, and going to Camp Loma Mar. Blanche's theory worked for Thomas, as he was out of the house; but, once indoors, human laws prevailed—In Thomas's home environment the conditions were all fight; all blame.

The Sixth Piece:
Shaped by Interactions within Cultural and Societal Institutions

Kindergarten

Kindergarten was Thomas's first introduction to the second of society's bedrock institutions: public school education. In 1944-45 the rigorous K-curriculum encompassed play, schoolwork, milk and gram crackers, and a noontime nap. Thomas finds himself thriving as the center of attention at Lafayette Elementary School.[dd] At home it's pretty much the same routine, fighting and screaming. Thomas learns and loves school. He is growing to be more assertive, more independent, more demanding, more inquisitive, more verbal, and more active. Up at 6:00 A.M. until 8:00 P.M. bedtime, his motor is running at full speed. "Thomas floored us this evening, when he sang the first song he learned in Kindergarten: "Choo, Choo, Choo." (10/26/44) This is the only mention of school during Thomas's kindergarten year. In this case no news can be considered good news. Evidently things went well and Thomas would come home and entertain his parents with what he learned at school.

Blanche and the ghost decided to move Thomas from public school into the nearby parochial school, Saint Francis de Sales, a private institution of learning. Although there is no record as to why the move was made, a look at the racial make up of Thomas's kindergarten class is telling. Also, Blanche is convinced that Thomas will have a better education at Saint Francis where the Sisters of the Holy Names will watch him more carefully—just like his mother would watch him. Thomas was a problem child at home and, by Jove, he wasn't going to become a problem at school. Keep this kid on a short leash, and everything will turn out well.

First Grade

Blanche writes less and less about Thomas in *Our Baby Book*; but there is a clear information trail showing how he progressed through eight years of parochial elementary school. Less than a month into the first grade, and the dye was cast.

> "We are having a terrible time with Thomas at school. He will not apply himself to studies; all he thinks about is play. Sister Stephen insists he is very intelligent and should be able to learn without much effort but his little mind just wander...at present things look bad for promotion to the second grade." (November 2, 1945)

> "Thomas's foolin' around in class and kicked his shoe off, Sister Stephan Mary picked up his shoe and put it in her pocket." (April 11, 1946)

Blanche's November 2, 1945 entry becomes a mantra, which was sung every year by every teacher Thomas ever had. What is wrong with Thomas? On March 6, 1946, Sister Stephen Mary gave her first grade class an art and language assignment on the topic, "Work Your Father Is Doing." Thomas drew a picture of his dad embalming a body that was subtitled, "Make work your father is doing 8:30 for St. Thomas."[hh] The "8:30 for St. Thomas" phrase referred to having the body embalmed, dressed, in its casket, with hair combed, made up, and rolling into Saint Thomas's Church at 8:30 in the morning. Hugh Rosen's study of children's drawings show such drawings to follow similar age-related patterns of development regardless of culture or geography.[28]

Children ages four through seven typically have no problems drawing story or sentence pictures and can explain the meaning of every object and figure in the drawing.[29] Obviously, the particulars drawn by Thomas are familiar to him, as he explained them to his first grade classmates. Within the framed picture Thomas showed his father, wearing a protective apron, while he embalmed a dead body. The body is laid out on the morgue room table with its head propped up on what Thomas knows as a "rubber pillow". A glass container filled with embalming fluid hangs from the ceiling and is connected by a rubber tube to the body. Gravity pushes the embalming fluid through the tube into the arteries and veins of the deceased until the individual's blood has been replaced with the preservative fluid. The object on the floor behind his dad is the gutbucket, the container where the internal organs of the deceased are placed while his dad does the cavity work. Thomas draws a long neck on the cadaver, as he knows dad has to insert the embalming needle into the carotid artery and has to insert a draining needle into the jugular vein on the side of the neck. The tubes from the overhead embalming fluid container go into the chest indicating that his dad is embalming a person who has been autopsied.

Thomas has incorporated into his drawing: hair on the top of his father's head and some facial features of his dad and the corpse. Notice that the body has no clothes. The picture appears realistic and seems to have been drawn with a firm hand. There exist no classic warning signs of troubled children, such as shaky lines, repeated forms, slanted images, glaringly immature drawing or certain objects being drawn in distinctly immature manners.[30] Thomas, as far as the picture tells, is a normal, observant, intelligent child with age appropriate motor development.

So, while Thomas is struggling along through the first grade, there are no signs that he is a slow learner, inept, or overwhelmed by school.

Second Grade

"We have quite a time with him. He almost refused to study, just wants to play all the time when he adapts himself his marks are excellent, when not in the mood to do things, his marks are terrible. (April 24, 1947)

Third Grade

"We're having quite a time with Thomas, he just absolutely refuses to apply himself to schoolwork or anything worth while, except funny books, Kiddie Shows, guns and play of all kinds." (March 28, 1948)

Fourth Grade

"I had to go to school and give Thomas a licking. My Gosh, when is he going to settle down, he" drive me to drink." (October 26, 1948)

"Thomas is sure a bad egg when it comes to studying his school work. Ye Gads! (November 1, 1948)

Fifth Grade

"He won't study at school, everything is play and all he thinks about is fighting and guns." (January 29, 1950)

Sixth Grade

There is no record of Thomas in the sixth grade.

Seventh Grade

"Thomas is in the 7th grade, forgot his manners in the cafeteria, and had to write the following note to his Dad to be signed and returned to the principal: Dear dad, I was putting beans on the end of my spoon, and by hitting the other end I shot it up in the air in the cafeteria. s/Thomas Greenstone." (January 8, 1952)

Eighth Grade

"Thomas is absolutely a character in school, if he used his head for his studies like he does for his foolishness, he would be a genius. Day-in-day-out, year-in-year-out, same old story, study, study, study, and he fights all of us, but boy is he good with his alibis and excuses, and he has plenty of them. He is now in the 8th grade and we're all still after him to study." (March 20, 1953)

"Thomas graduated from St. Francis de Sales." (June 11, 1953, 7:30 PM)

By 1945, Japan, Germany, and Italy had surrendered to the United States and its allied powers to end the Second World War. In 1953, the Korean conflict ended in an armistice between the United States and North Korea; but the war between Thomas and Blanche continued.

Saint Elizabeth High School

Thomas had serious knowledge gaps[31] in reading, writing, and arithmetic that negatively impacted his overall academic progress in school. At home Thomas had incredible pressures on him to behave and succeed. Years of criticism, physical punishment, removal from class, and childhood illness had taken their toll. He had advanced from elementary to high school, but his learning gaps and poor study habits caught up with him. At the end of his freshman year Blanche and Sam were informed that Thomas could not return to Saint Elizabeth in the fall of 1954.

Oakland Technical High School

You can be assured that Thomas's reputation preceded him every where he went in the parochial school system; but it did not follow him into public high school. As a sophomore at Tech, Thomas was an unknown. He had no history. Thomas was liberated from his "problem child" reputation at school. And, his home situation had improved, as Thomas was out of the house as much as possible, thereby reducing contact between him and Blanche. At Tech Thomas's grades would not qualify him to enter a four-year college. They were over all barely passable, and in some cases his grades were excellent.

<u>"C-/D+" English (three years including Public Speaking)</u>: Thomas was in the college prep classes and found English tough sledding.

<u>"D" History (three years)</u>: A subject heavily dependent on reading and reading comprehension. Thomas had difficulty.

<u>"C-" Algebra (I and II)</u>: Algebra is built on arithmetic, which Thomas did not fully understand, but he liked the subject.

<u>"A" Geometry</u>: An "A"! What happened here? Two factors come into play. First, Thomas was "wounded" by criticism and got off on the wrong foot in school; he was not "stupid". If a student has difficulty with arithmetic, trouble with algebra soon follows. When Thomas took Geometry there was no link to arithmetic or algebra. Consequently, Geometry was a brand new subject for Thomas, which began by learning axioms and postulates (the A-B-C's of geometry) and moved forward in a logical manner from the simple to the more complex. Thomas hadn't miss out on the basics of geometry, therefore, he had no learning gaps.[35] Second, the teacher, Max Ulich, was a gifted teacher, who was well suited for Thomas. Max had a dry-sarcastic, but never critical or demeaning, sense of humor that resembled Sam's sense of humor. Max Ulich posed interesting problems for his students to ponder. Thomas rediscovered his joy of learning. He "discovers he can do things and does he get a bang out of it," as Blanche observed back on January 7, 1941. (NOTE: Observing a child who has had trouble in school blossom in a subject or activity (e.g., successfully takes up chess, learns to speak Chinese), which is not related to prior learning, indicates not only that the child is bright and resilient, but that, just maybe, a number of his key teachers failed, for some reason, to reach him or her.)

"C" Science (biology, chemistry, physics): Thomas's interest was high, but his poor reading skills took their toll.

"D-" Spanish (I-VII): Double Ouch! The learning of Spanish or other romance languages are linked to how well a child understands English. Thomas's Spanish teacher, Ms. Betzner, cut a deal with Thomas. If Thomas didn't take Spanish VIII, she would give him a D-, which was barely passing in those days. Thomas jumped at the deal and took Boys Chorus.

"C" High School Reserved Officer Training Corps (in lieu of Physical Education): Perfect! Fair discipline and advancement based on achievement. Thomas found ROTC highly motivating, even though his grades were average. ROTC involved reading, but also included target practice, marching, aggressor force training, and special drill team advancement.

"A" Mechanical Drawing (one year): No reading, spatial/analytical and detailed. Another new start, another success.

"B" Boys' Chorus (one semester): Thomas loved to sing and had a reasonably good voice, but boys' will be boys.

Thomas went on to graduate from high school with a 1.7 (D+) grade point average. Thank god for community colleges! Thomas graduated from a four year college and eventually earned his doctorate—the classic "late bloomer".

Blanche's penultimate entry in *Our Baby Book* reads:

> "THOMAS IS 15 & 1/2 YEARS OLD AND IS IMPOSSIBLE TO HAN-
> DLE. HE ABSOLUTELY REFUSES TO COOPERATE. HE THINKS HE
> KNOWS EVERYTHING AND REFUSES TO LEARN." (April 1955)

Blanche has given up on Thomas and is unaware of the positive changes that are shaping Thomas at school, changes that demonstrate his ability to learn quite well. Also, Blanche is unaware of Thomas's leadership abilities that are being shaped in school clubs (i.e., Junior Achievement, ROTC Rifle Team, and Special Drill Team). And, Blanche is unaware of the benefit that Thomas is reaping from two other community institutions—the Oakland Central YMCA and Oakland Neighborhood Church.

The Oakland YMCA

Based on Blanche's theory that living in the small apartment was the major reason for Thomas's problems, Thomas was enrolled in the YMCA after school program in 1948. Blanche never realized how much her strategy for Thomas worked, as few entries about the YMCA and YMCA Camp are recorded in *Our Baby Book*.

> "JULY 20, 1948—Thomas joined the YMCA, 8 years old."

> "JULY 1948—Thomas went to the Oakland YMCA Camp located in Loma Mar."

> "NOVEMBER 13, 1948—Thomas is 9 years old and attended his 1st football game with the YMCA boys, California vs. Washington State."

Blanche's comments about Thomas's involvement in the YMCA stop after he was nine years old. As was chronicled by Dr. Greenstone in Part II and as was verified by newspaper articles, the YMCA developed Thomas's leadership skills and athletic abilities, provided inspiration and motivation for success, and opened opportunities for Thomas to earn money year round. Thomas was recognized in the Oakland Tribune Newspaper many times as a swim team member, swim instructor, life guard, program director, Red Cross Drown-proofing volunteer (for disabled children), and YMCA Camp Counselor. The influence of the YMCA shaped Thomas's life from age eight through twenty-one, when Thomas graduated from college.

Junior Achievement

Blanche did not mention Junior Achievement because her last entry in *Our Baby Book* was April 25, 1955 and Thomas was in Junior Achievement during his junior and senior high school years. As was discussed in Part II, according to Dr. Greenstone's recollection, Junior Achievement gave him the opportunity to succeed and be recognized for his accomplishments. His parents, Blanche and Sam, attended the Junior Achievement dinner at the Oakland Lemington Hotel and were quite proud of him. I imagine that the time for keeping records of Thomas's achievements had passed Blanche by. Or, maybe Blanche figured that Thomas was grown up and on his own, and was no longer her responsibility.

In any case, Thomas's participation in Junior Achievement at Oakland Tech was one of the high points of his high school experience.

Oakland Neighborhood
(Spiritual Matters)

Sometime in 1955, Thomas's old West Oakland friend, Jerry Guerino,ᵒᵒ was living in East Oakland, when he invited Thomas to go to a new church next to Castlemont High School. Thomas was a Catholic, who had interacted with a wide variety of priests, ministers, rabbi's, and atheists at the mortuary, and had no bias against protestant churches. Like the kids at Tech, the kids at Neighboorhood Church accepted Thomas at face value. No hurdles to jump; no "in groups" to become part of. Thomas was unconditionally accepted as a fellow child of God—good medicine. In short time, Thomas became a different person than he was at home. In the face of love and no criticism there were no fights and no blame. Hundreds of kids Thomas's age were in Omega, the high school group at Neighborhood Church. There were dinners, picnics, and all kinds of social events. Oakland Neighborhood Church was another home away from home that would further hone Thomas's moral views and practices. Convinced he was the cause of all the trouble at home and that he was at fault for his poor school performance, the message he heard at Neighborhood Church was overwhelmingly powerful. "All have sinned and come short of the glory of God and this horrendous burden of sin that we all carry can be removed for all time…You are forgiven by Christ who loved you before the beginning of time." Ken Backlund, the youth minister, who delivered the message, was an honest, straightforward, charismatic personality that seemed to be speaking directly to Thomas, as he sat in the Omega service that Sunday morning. Thomas accepted Christ. He continued the long journey of thinking before he spoke and attempting to think and act as Christ would have thought and acted in the same situation; and his life began to change for the better. Like Saul being knocked off his ass on the way to Damascus, Thomas was floored by his spiritual awaking. Thomas had become a new person.

Back home Blanche, a non-practicing Roman Catholic, expresses concern about this Protestant Church. Thomas answered that Jerry was there and he liked going to the church. "But you're a Roman Catholic Thomas; you went to parochial school; what about that?" Thomas told his mother that he was still Catholic. All that Thomas did was to go to confession and accept Christ just like he was taking communion at Mass. Except at Neighborhood Church, Thomas understood what communion was all about. As far as Thomas was concerned Protestants were Catholics that didn't know Latin.

Sam was an atheist and a Congregationalist who believed one's relationship with God was a private and personal matter between that person and God. Thomas's new home at Neighborhood Church connected with both his Roman Catholic education and his Congregational leanings. The Omega high school group at Neighborhood Church, like the YMCA, offered leadership opportunities and helped Thomas's confidence and ability to speak to groups of people. It is interesting that all this rebuilding of Thomas was taking place as his mother predicted. For Thomas to improve his behavior, he needed to get out of the cramped quarters of the apartment.

The Seventh Piece:
Shaped By Interactions with Others
(It takes a village…)

There were always other adults in Thomas's life that loved him and developed positive relationships with him. Charlene, Blanche's girlfriend; Mary and Virgil Caporgno, Thomas's Godparents; Mrs. Arnold, Caporgno and Company receptionist, Bea Stewart, secretary, Scotty, Grandma Frietas, Grandpa Joe, Auntie Snelgrove, Katherine, and Inez Greenstone, Sam's brother's wife. It is clear from the record that Mary Caporgno and Charlene socialized with Blanche on a frequent basis, gave Blanche morale support, and discussed how to raise Thomas. In many ways the mortuary environment was an extended family with up to as many as nine or ten people working with Sam and socializing with Blanche and Thomas on a daily basis.

Outside of the mortuary and outside the family, there were the others that added to Thomas's life, which served to keep him on the straight and narrow.

Louie and Cleda Guerino: The Guerino's were the parents of Thomas's good friend Jerry, whom he met at the YMCA around 1952. Thomas was captivated by the healthy dynamics within the Guerino family, where he was always made to feel like one of the family. (1952–2004)

Gus McKinnon: The YMCA Secretary and Swim Team Coach, who worked with Thomas from 1948 through 1957. The man was a fine Christian male role model who enjoyed kids, supported their physical and emotional development, and provided opportunities for them to serve and lead.

Sister Mary Dorothea: When all had failed in finding the key to turn on Thomas's abilities to learn and contribute, Sister Dorothea found the key and opened the lock: Thomas would do anything given the responsibility to serve. (1953)

Wayne Cockrell: The YMCA Camp Loma Mar Director, who worked closely with Thomas. Wayne was the first person to teach Thomas to grow up through the use of natural consequences. He suspended Thomas from working at Camp Loma Mar for one summer. He also accepted him back the following summer. Wayne was a fair man that didn't suffer fools. (1955–1960)

Reverend Ken Backlund: Assistant Pastor and Youth Minister for Oakland Neighborhood Church, a college athlete and charismatic personality whose down-to-earth nature and devotion to Christ guided many teenagers, especially boys, on the right path through adolescence. (1955–1957)

Dr. John Robinson: College professor who took a personal interest in Thomas and took great care in guiding Thomas through college to graduation. (1959-1961)

Peter Hanson: Thomas's master teacher in the Jefferson Elementary School District, who brought Thomas home nights and weekends to literally tutor him in the art of teaching.

What did these folks have that drew Thomas to them like a bee to honey? Thomas would have walked through fire to please them. Why? Posed with these questions Dr. Greenstone looked puzzled at first and then jotted down several characteristics shared by all of them. They:

• Never criticized or swore.

• Never touched Thomas, except in a caring, affirming manner.

• Used conversation, silence, and/or natural consequences as the means of guiding, correcting, and/or triggering Thomas's to thinking.

• Spent lots of time in two-way conversations with Thomas.

• Seemed to value Thomas and his opinions.

• Were forthright in speech and action.

Although these people outside of Thomas's family had different personalities, different life styles, and different beliefs, they seemed to follow the same script.

> "Love is patient and kind; it is not jealous or conceited or proud; love is not ill mannered or selfish or irritable; love does not keep a record of wrongs; love is not happy with evil, but is happy with the truth. Love never gives up; and its faith, hope, and patience never fail."[32]

These adults made a powerful difference in Thomas's life. During much of childhood and early youth, Thomas was under sustained attack at home and at school, which could have severely warped his view of life, more than it is. The Greenstone household tended to be a war zone at all times. In the *Leviathan*, Thomas Hobbs once wrote about when government and society fails to provide for the security of the individual:

> "In such conditions there is no place for industry, because the fruit thereof is uncertain…no knowledge of the face of the earth; no account of time; no arts; no letters…and worst of all, continual fear, and danger of violent death; and the life of man solitary, poor, nasty, brutish, and short."[33]

In the emotionally volatile environments of home and school Thomas found life to be uncertain. His efforts at home and school were unproductive. He fell short at school, acquiring little knowledge of geography, telling time, and art appreciation or written language. At times in his early years life seemed to be nasty, brutish, and for all he knew, short. As an only child in a hostile environment, he was in solitude. While in formal situations he could behave in a polite, engaging, and intelligent manner, vile language and a strike-response mentality always lurked beneath the surface of his best behavior. In informal situations, especially with peers, he was outspoken, argumentative, and articulate with a peppering of foul language. Thomas's swearing was often a litmus test. If the individual with whom Thomas was talking could comfortably handle Thomas's language, then Thomas felt accepted and would risk further contact with the person. But if Thomas's uncouth manner repelled the individual, then a natural selection would take place, resulting in the other person going away. In time Thomas would have hardened this litmus test into his personality and his worldview would have been indistinguishable from that of Thomas Hobbs. Fortunately, others in Thomas's life were positive and accepted him just as he was, counterbalancing the harsh treatment he found at home and in his early schooling.

The Eighth Piece:
Thinks, Wonders, Questions, Tinkers, Learns Exercises
Free Will, Creates, and Destroys

It is clear to this writer that newborn babies are as perfect as human's get on this side of the mortal veil. It is equally clear that it's the parents and society that tend to mess things up—something that animal parents tend not to do. Animals think, tinker, create, and destroy—the natural order of things in the wild. The chimpanzee that pokes a stick through a hole in a termite mound to bring up a fresh meal illustrates this point. Thinking, tinkering, and creating ways to survive, animals create minimal destruction to their environments and their species.

Born 24 December 1920 in Edgard, Louisiana, Dave Bartholomew grew up to write and arrange numerous Delta Blues hits with Fats Domino, including "Ain't it a Shame," "I'm in Love Again," "Blue Monday," and "I'm Walkin'" to mention a very few. But the Blues classic that summed up the differences between mankind and the "lower animals" was a little song entitled "The Monkey".

> "Three monkeys sat in a coconut tree
> Discussing things as they are said to be.
> One said to the other, 'Listen here, you two.
> I just heard a rumor that CAN'T be true.'
> 'That man descended from our noble race!
> The very idea is a big disgrace.
> No monkey ever cheated his wife,
> Starved her baby, and ruined her life.'
> Yeah.
> The monkey speaks his mind!
>
> 'You'll never see a mother monk
> Leave her child with others to bunk.
> Passing him off from one to the other,
> Till the poor child barely knows his own mother.'
> Yeah.
> The monkey speaks his mind!

'And here's another thing you'll never see—
A monkey build a fence around a coconut tree.
Letting good coconuts go to waste
While forbidding all others to come and taste.
Why, if I built a fence around a tree,
Starvation would force you to steal from me.'
Yeah.
The monkey speaks his mind!

'And here's one more thing a monkey won't do—
Go out at night and get on a stew.
Or use a gun, or club, or knife
To take another monkey's life.
Yes, man descended, the worthless bum.
But brothers, from us HE DID NOT COME.'
Yeah.
The monkey speaks his mind!"

Humans, by virtue of well-developed forebrains, tend to move beyond the natural order of things in the wild, as they wonder, question, and exercise free will; and humans create maximum destruction to their environments and harm their species, including their own children. This tendency of humans to screw things up to a fare-the-well continues to run rampant through out human societal institutions and society in general. Ah, we are an arrogant people; to wit:

Last week, I heard a sad news story.[34] Scientists from the Rosilin Institute revealed, "Dolly, the world's first cloned sheep, was euthanized after being diagnosed with progressive lung disease." Only six years earlier, Scottish scientists had announced that Dolly, a lamb, had been produced from a micro-surgically altered sheep's egg. The hereditary material in the original egg was replaced by nucleus material from another sheep's cells and implanted in the ewe—no ram was needed.[35] Dolly had a mother, but no father. I didn't lightly consider the fact that this news was announced on Valentine's Day.[34] More recently the Dolly people announced that by utilizing animal stem cells there is no need for a male or a female to create the eggs and sperm necessary to create new life.[36] So much for the natural order of things; and proof positive that we didn't descend from the monkey.

Two weeks ago, I was listening to Science Friday on the car radio and caught the tail end of a discussion about the Human Genome Project. Evidently, genetic scientists have completed the gnomic sequencing of the human cell's twenty-three chromosomes and have further opened the door to human manipulation of human genetic materials. Genetic engineering holds the hope of eliminating cancer, drug and alcohol addictions, mental illnesses such as schizophrenia and other diseases and conditions that plague the human race.[37] But, such scientific advancement also bring risks that someone or some group will misapply the knowledge, using it in unethical ways or using the information to create monsters—Frankenstein, another myth turned reality. The United States Congress is all a twitter, and rightfully so, about the probable misuse of genetic research to clone human dolly's or worse.

> "A bill banning all human cloning faces an uncertain future in the Senate after sailing through the House Thursday. The 241 to 155 vote came after lawmakers defeated a proposal to allow cloning for research to find cures for diseases like Parkinson's and Alzheimer's. Proponents of the House bill have conceded they do have the 60 votes necessary in the Senate to end debate and force a vote on the legislation. The bill would ban all human cloning—for reproduction or research—and impose a one million dollar fine and a prison sentence of up to 10 years for violators."[38]

Then there are the Raelian Revolution folks who believe they are gods and want to break the good news on us now. The Revolution's message to us is:

> "We were the ones who made all life on earth." You mistook us for gods."
> "We now reveal to you the secret behind the main religions."[39]

Raelians believe that cloning is the path to everlasting life; and they are in England, far from the jurisdiction of the U.S. Congress. Can't you just hear the monkeys saying, "Yes, man descended, the worthless bum. But brothers, from us HE DID NOT COME."

> Rael continues, "Today's new cloning technology is the first step in the quest for immortality or eternal life. What past religions used to promise only after death in a mythical paradise will soon be a scientific reality on earth—this is Rael's challenging conclusion in an incisive and wide-ranging view of how science is about to revolutionise all our lives. Once we can clone exact replicas of ourselves, the next step will be to transfer our memory and personality into our newly cloned brains and this will allow us to truly live forever."

> "The Raelian Revolution, the world's largest UFO related, non-profit organisation—over 60,000 members in 90 countries—working towards the first embassy to welcome people from space...sweeping the world with the most

politically incorrect and fearlessly individualistic philosophy of non-conform-ism."[39]

I don't think this dog will hunt. I'm sure stranger ideologies have appeared and disappeared throughout the course of time, but I can't recall when that might have been. I'd rather worship an Egyptian dung beetle. Paleontologists tell us that the only certainty we face as a species is extinction. If Rael takes hold, we will be making the last turn towards perdition—Saints preserve us.

A Man Has to Know His Limitations

Nature continues to present mankind with perfect learning machines with each human birth. Newborn human children, having all their fingers and toes, are genetically hardwired with a sophisticated intelligence, logical understanding, curiosity, and all the tools required to explore and learn from its environment. Humankind is blessed with incredible free will, with which "lower animals" aren't terribly burdened. But the blessing comes with the responsibility to follow our better instincts. Our most primitive instincts tell us to think, wonder, ques-tion, learn, and create. Man also has the capacity to destroy what has been cre-ated. When choices to destroy are presented, man's choice needs to be tempered by his knowledge of his own limitations. This is especially true, when parents commit to create a child. That some parents need to have their infants come into this world with a factory sticker, which says, "Don't bend or break, under penalty of having a mill stone tied around your neck and drowned in the deepest sea" is a sad commentary to make.[40] Harsh and brutish, violent behavior towards children is "soul murder." [41] Parents, teachers, and all members in a society have a moral imperative to understand the dynamics of cycles of family violence and to elimi-nate the causes of family violence, starting with our own families.

The Ninth Piece:
Throughout Life, has the Capacity
to Reinvent Her or Himself

None of us, reading this story, has poor enough protoplasm or bad enough genet-ics avoid being able to reinvent ourselves at any given moment—it's a matter of will, however, some people need a boost to get going. For some it's a religious experience. For others, it's stepping back to take a good look at the state of our existence. Others change because of tragic events, taking place in their lives. And still others come about without giving the matter a second thought in the course of their busy, busy lives.

We are not predestined by our genetics or by the conditions in which we find ourselves. James Watson, whose discovery, along with Crick, celebrated the 50th year of their discovering the double helix in 1953. In his recent book, DNA, The Secret of Life,[42] conjectures that a "violence gene" may be found one day; and that that finding may show how aggressive behavior traits pass from one generation to another. However, Watson goes on to say, if a genetic link to violence does exist, it still does not determine that the individual will necessarily exhibit over the top aggressive behaviors. Why? Because if genetics did fix our destinies, we would not be communicating in a variety of ways, as we are in this book, our species could not have adapted to the range of environments in which it currently finds itself (e.g., arctic regions, hot humid equatorial jungles, bottoms of oceans, space), and the mention of free will would receive the response: Huh? So, humans clearly have the capacity to change, to reinvent themselves at any time,

Our genetics do predispose us to act certain ways, as we interact within our environment, which even furthers the case for free will over genetic predestination. Our genes are designed in such a way, as to have us make joint choices in our lives—just me and my environment, babe. And, my guess is that the choices that genetics pushes us to make are healthy choices, which preserve our survival and the survival of our families and tribes. Consequently, being predisposed by our genetics to do healthy choices is hardly an intolerably restriction on my free will to choose to change or reinvent myself.

But, God/god is all-knowing; we can't make a free choice other than what God/god knows we will make. You may be right. Free will may well be an illusion, but, until we see God/god and know God/god as we are known, it's kind of silly to give up the ghost, when free will seems to work so well and holds the hope that if humans start to clean-up their acts, especially when they become parents, human potential will be actualized, never before. Besides, God/god revealed that we do have free will. Is God/god a liar?

But, my family has always lived in poverty; and I'm caught capitalist vortex that sweeps my free will to change into the gutters of every city. Yes, there are conditions we find overwhelming. If such thinking isn't a recurring precursor to a coming epiphany, which will reinvent that individual, I don't know what is. We all have choices to make in our environments, aided by our healthy-leaning genetics and our God/god revelations about free will, but not everyone will make the right choices and become eaten up within cycles of self and family destruction. However, all of our life experiences tell us that when we start giving excuses, blaming others and conditions for our inability to change, we are fooling ourselves.

The message here is short and clear: we have no excuse for being a lousy parents, grandparents, and great grandparents; and if we are lousy, we know, and need to change.

The Tenth Piece:
May Mate with Another Genetic-Self

Family records reveal our personal histories and answer key questions about how we arrived where we are in the present. Bring this information to a conscious level allows us to understand our places in the family life cycle and to more effectively act in behalf of our families' best interests in the time remaining in our lives. Even a mere listing of part of our family trees gives us some insight into how life operates. For example, Thomas's lineage on his father's side reads as follows.

John Thomas Greenstone (b. 1862, est.)
Married
Alice Mildred Birdwistle (b. 1862, est.)

Philip Mathew Greenstone (1880–1942)
Married
Margaret E. Hurst (1886–1945)

Samuel Taylor Greenstone (1910-1971)
Married
Blanche Mary Frietas (1907–1968)

Thomas Zechariah Greenstone (1939–)
Married
Marie Helen Castellanos (1936–)

Michael Taylor Greenstone (1968–)
Currently not married

Jason Allen Adams (1969–)
Married
Kimberly Marie Greenstone (1967–)

Megan Makena Adams (2003–)

This one hundred forty-two-year abbreviated genealogy reveals to Thomas where he is in the web of life and what opportunities open to him presently. Now in his mid-sixties and retired, Thomas has many opportunities to enjoy, even to indulge himself in the good life. Marie loves to travel—so there will be traveling to new places in old countries. Thomas has never had difficulty entertaining himself. Every interest that catches Thomas's fancy becomes a mini-obsession and, in time, fades into his garage. His garage is a testament, or a graveyard, to past and reoccurring adventures—skiing, martial arts, arachnology, bowling balls, golf, entomology, gardening, zoology, poker, guitars, books, back-packing, tinkering-projects, and on and on. But, the pinnacle adventure of his life to date, was the news from his daughter that a granddaughter was on her way and that Michael, her brother, was to be the godfather. In an epiphanic He still had many interests, but now he could share those interests with his granddaughter, who would find everything new and exciting. Now, Thomas's passion is to help Marie take care of baby Megan, as often as possible. And, in taking care of Megan, the wonder of life unfolding began again.

Megan Makena Adams

On June 21, 2000 Kimberly Marie Greenstone (1967) and Jason Allen Adams (1969) were married in Hawaii. Born on June 16, 2003, Megan Makena Adams, the Sierra star, rose high above Sacramento California, becoming the next generation of the Greenstone family.

Thursday, October 16, 2003: Megan is four months old, to the day.[jj] Her grandparents have been babysitting for three days, while Kim was at a cadaver lab at Stanford University. The little tyke is fourteen and one-half pounds (just a half a pound short of a bowling ball) and approximately twenty-three inches long. Around the clock she provides grandparents and parents with grand opportunities to observe, care for, love, and enjoy her, as she ventures into the world. According to Thomas and Chess, a newborn's behavior fluctuates from hour-to-hour, day-to-day, and does not settle into a reliable pattern. By the second or third months of life, whatever predictable pattern the baby has is established and observable.[43] Consequently, below, we have a 4-month time lapse shot of Megan's temperament using the work of Thomas and Chess as a discussion guide.

Megan's Temperamental Constellation

Temperamental Characteristics	Observations
1 Rhythmicity (predictability)	<u>Regular</u>: You can usually set your watch by Megan's schedule: Wakes up happy as a clam at 8:00ish and has her diaper changed; plays by herself until fed 4 to 6 oz. of milk. 8:30ish plays on stomach (Tummy Time Gym), plays on back 'til 9:00ish and watches Baby Bach on the DVD until 9:30ish. Goes outside for a walk around the block, held by a parent or grandparent for an half an hour or so, plays, sits in her "chickie chair" and watches Rollie Pollie Ollie at 10:00 A.M., diaper change, then is fed 4 to 6 oz. of milk at 10:30ish. Megan rocks in her Ocean-sounds swing with fish, clam, and starfish and seahorse mobile turning above her and her felt-toy animals in hand (horse and duck). She is walked around the house, laid in her crib, where she plays with another musical mobile and randomly kicks, activating another ocean-scene/musical toy that is clipped to her crib; Between 11:00 A.M., and Noon Megan is picked up and walked in the master bedroom, dark with drapes drawn, sometimes fusses, sometimes throws a fit, sometimes zonks right out and is placed in the middle of the master bed, sucking her left thumb and feels the top of her head with her right hand and naps for more or less than two to three hours, which usually brings her to around to 2:00 to 3:00 in the afternoon, when she wakes up happy as a clam, gooing and all. She is changed and cleaned (usually the first poop of the day, which resembles guacamole or a lemon to peach sorbet). She is up and ready to rock and roll. Megan has her early afternoon play session as in the morning. Watches Baby Bach, a Disney feature, CSPN, a great way to calm the baby, watches ESPN, and the Entertainment Channel, the World Series (Marlins v. Yankees), college and pro football, and other sports of every stripe. She goes outside for a walk, "reads" her favorite and only book, "Hush Little Alien", has a diaper change, is ready for her afternoon feeding of 6 to 8 oz. of milk at about 6:30 P.M., and goes through the pre-sleep ritual until sound asleep at 7:30ish. At night she wakes up at about 2:00 A.M., happy as a clam, has her diaper changed, and drinks about 6 oz. of milk. Then it's the pre-sleep routine until 3:00ish, sleeps, plays 'till 8:00ish, and starts all over again—happy as a clam.

2	Approach or Withdrawal Response	<u>Approach</u>: Whether it's a new toy, food, person, event or situation Megan reacts positively as evidenced by mood, expression, actions, and sometimes verbalizations.
3	Adaptability (new stimuli)	<u>Adaptive</u>: Easily adaptable to new experiences. Even when scared at first, like when her Uncle (and Godfather) Michael, wide-eyed and gleefully pushed a large-round, brightly colored plastic dog-toy that barked loudly and vibrated, into Megan's stomach, Megan eventually warmed up to the dog-toy after crying and settling down—an event that Uncle Michael will always be shell-shocked about, which speaks volumes about Michael's adaptability.
4	Quality Of Mood (amount of pleasant or unpleasant behavior)	<u>Positive</u>: Happy as a clam 94% of the time she is awake, but occasionally fussy or fitful before bedtime 4% of the time. (Based on an eleven and one half-hour waking day.)
5	Activity Level (wiggle factor)	<u>Medium</u>: Megan is clam and engages parent by eye-contact when being fed, bathed, dressed, changed, or given toys to play with. She is restless (arching her back and wriggling) when she has had enough of sitting or laying in the same place. Megan is calm and attentive watching Baby Bach and Rollie Pollie Ollie, and when taken for a walk or is out in the back yard. She loves to look at trees and reaches for and grasps twigs and leaves. Megan becomes visibly excited (eyes widen and she bounces around with glee) when Hush Little Alien is read to her and when she is kicking her crib toys and watching mobiles.
6.	Threshold of Responsiveness (evoke response)	<u>Medium</u>: A touch or a gentle poke doesn't produce a pronounced response from Megan, but she is easily stimulated by interactions with others. When she sees her baby bottle or when someone places a finger towards her mouth, Megan gives them a "shark attack" response—mouth wide opened as if ready to chomp down. Handling the baby produces eye contact, as she watches everything going on.
7	Intensity Of Reaction (energy level)	<u>Variable</u>: Megan's expenditure of energy depends on the situation. High energy is expended during times of bedtime fussiness and excitement during play or while some one is reading to her. Otherwise, she is calm and observant about everything else.

8	Environmental Distraction Level	<u>No</u>: Extraneous environmental stimuli do not interfere with or alter the direction of Megan's behavior. When she is watching and listening to Baby Bach or playing with her toys. Kitchen noise, the cats parading by, or adult conversations or activities do not distract Megan. Likewise, when Megan is occupying herself or watching the cats, she is not distracted by the television or other happenings around the house.
9a	Persistence (continuation)	<u>Yes</u>: Megan persists in the face of obstacles preventing her from what she wants to do. If she is reaching for a tree limb, flower, the cat, or her toys, pushing her arm down or standing in the way will not stop her from continuing her activity.
9b	Attention Span (length of time)	<u>Yes</u>: Megan displays long periods of attention when observing the out of doors, watching television, playing with mobiles, and the like.

Analysis

At four months, Megan's behavior is characterized by regularity, positive approach responses to new stimuli, high adaptability to change moderately intense moods, which are preponderantly positive. She quickly developed a regular feeding schedule, took to new foods easily, smiled at strangers, adapted easily to new situations, and accepted most frustration (except around sleeping time) with little fuss. She accepts adults holding her, changing her, setting limitations to her movements. Thomas and Chess would classify Megan as an "Easy Child"—one who is a joy to her parents, pediatricians, and others around her. "Easy Children" comprised about 40% of their New York Longitudinal Study sample.[44]

"So far so good," as Blanche would say. Just remember that raising Megan is not like running a 100-meter dash; it's a life-long marathon. Your next marathon with child #2 may be with a perfectly good "Difficult Child" who enhances your parenting capacity, stretching you to be even more creative, positive, and insightful parents. Remember these "Difficult Children" do grow up to be remarkable adults, if parented well and are lucky along the way. Are your appetites whetted for # 3 child? Yes? No? Maybe that's why on average there are only 2.4 children produced per family in the United States.[kk]

<u>Thursday, November 27, 2003</u>: Megan's first Thanksgiving Day was spent at Grandma and Grandpa's house. Kim is at work, flying around the Bay Area, while Jason shares his Mr. Mom duties with the grandparents. Megan, at five months and eleven days old has fully developed what Blanche called a "striking personality". Megan's version of a striking personality is to make growling noises

mingled with gleeful high pitched sounds, as she attacks you with her mouth wide open, shaking her head from sided to side before she lunges to bite your finger or neck. The family is hysterical with laughter, as Megan continually repeats her famous "shark attack". Megan's attack is reminiscent of Linda Blair's performance in *The Exorcist*, except Megan's head doesn't spin around quite as far as Linda—she does spit up, but only in an age-appropriate fashion! Megan is a very happy, outgoing, alert, and engaging baby, who enjoys life and is thoroughly enjoyed.[jj]

The Eleventh Piece:
Creates or Adopts Children or Chooses Not
to Continue the Human Life Cycle
Until Extinction Do They Part

I am persuaded that the extinction of the human species is based on the extinction of the human family unit. Destructive family environments tend to produce self-destructive progeny, which place future generations at risk. The good news is that positive family environments tend to create a positive, synergistic progeny, which better position future generations.

How does a family that is heading toward self-destruction and extinction change its course? One answer is by bringing new blood into the family. The marriage of Kim and Jason brings new blood into the Greenstone family. With different genetics and behaviors introduced into the family strain, old baggage, which has been carried from one generation to the next, may be lost, forgotten, or consciously removed, as life moves on.

But what does old family baggage look like? Obviously, the answer to this question is as varied as the number of families studied. And, old family baggage is mixed with good family traits, which make teasing out and identifying the old baggage difficult at times. Be that as it may, the following discussion is designed to tease out some of the negative family tapes and secrets, which will illustrate what constitutes old family baggage.

Family Tapes and Secrets

What family tapes and secrets were passed from Marie and Thomas to Kim and Michael's families? What family tapes and secrets were passed on from Al and Sharon (Jason's parents), to their son, Jason? And, when there are family tapes and secrets created in Jason, Kim, Michael (Uncle/Godfather), Ben (Uncle), and Diane (Second Cousin/Godmother) houses, will Kim, Jason, and the family have the wherewithal to correct behaviors and mitigate destructive affects before in midstream? Or, will family tapes and secrets be defended and ignored, allowing them to be dealt or not dealt with by the next generation, when Megan is in her mid-30s? The answer is clear in Thomas's mind—begin to unveil and end lousy family tapes and secrets, as early as possible. Of course for Thomas as soon as possible meant in his mid-sixties. With a bit of luck, Kim, Jason, Michael, Ben, and Diane will dispatch such matters sooner, and, as for Connie, hopefully, dispatching-time has come and gone. The payoff for a family's early engagement of abysmal tapes and secrets is not only to discontinue these deleterious practices, but to teach the young that stuff happens in all our lives, which must be confronted and not denied, and that, as a family, we are going to model for you and with you how to unscrew what is screw-up in a family—on the job training. So, in the interests of uncovering and exorcising some family demons from the Greenstone family, which is a hilarious notion given that family members are completely aware of these tapes and most family secrets, here's Thomas's appraisal.

Family Tapes

Family tapes come in three flavors: good, mixed, and bad. First, good family tapes, ones to be sustained generation after generation to ward off extinction of the family, position family members for probable prosperity and continuance.

Positioning refers to the ability of the parents to place in life to maximize their children's chances to succeed in their own lives. Positioning does not require that the children be placed in the "best" schools, with the "best" students, and have the "best" clothes and toys. Positioning requires that the children be placed in schools, community organizations and with friends that ensure high morale values, interaction with a diverse population of individuals and child-centered environments where acceptance, open expression, manners, and forgiveness abounded. Even parents who make monstrous mistakes with their children can position their children well. Blanche typifies this latter category.

Blanche was not a "good" mother in many respects, but her intentions were in the right place; and she tried hard. As the reader knows, early on in Thomas's life Blanche had figured the reason for Thomas's problems were that he did not have enough room to play and that he lived in a cramped apartment. So Blanche carefully positioned Thomas in places where this problem would be eliminated: vacations in the mountains and stays at the ranches and farms of relatives, after school activities at the YMCA, YMCA Camp, and lots of playtime outside of the house, including time with the Guerino family. Blanche was on the right track, but was on the wrong train. For positioning to be fully effective, parents need to observe and learn from the positive aspects of such positioning, which particularly and successfully enhance their children's lives, and incorporate these positive aspects into their family's day-to-day activities. Blanche did not think for a moment that she contributed to Thomas's problem. She denied her involvement in Thomas's problem so well that she was truly baffled at "bad" behaviors. So it was beyond her comprehension to study and take advantage of what she could have learned from Thomas's experiences, let alone incorporate such learning into the fabric of her family, as a family norm. Blanche and Sam's decision to place Thomas in a parochial school was motivated by the need to keep a close eye on his behavior and give him the best education they could. They missed on both counts, as Thomas's placement in parochial school, for the most part, only served to reinforce the negatives found in the Greenstone family, namely, continued identification of Thomas as the problem and the continued guidance of Thomas to the "right" path via physical punishment. At the time Thomas attended parochial school, the model set by many priests in the Catholic Church, which Thomas was exposed to at home in the mortuary and at school was that of a chain-smoking, alcohol drinking authoritarian figure, a perfect match between home and church.

Parents make major positioning decisions for their children almost every day. Family associations, child care, baby sitters, the parent's friends and their friends' children, school and teacher selections, after school activities, vacation choices, moral and spiritual learning, following up on interests expressed by their children, entertainment choices, exposing their children to new and different experiences, and most of all being a positive role model for their children all count as positioning choices for parents to make. These choices and more are very important parental decisions.

"Keeping Your Eye on the Prize" is another positive family trait, which needs to be sustained. This refers to the willingness and commitment of parents to place the child at the center of the family and to treat the child with great deference. Parents who keep their eyes on the prize know that their responsibility is to be a role model for the child in every way possible. One illustration: How do the mother and father communicate with each other? If the husband constantly ridicules and belittles the wife's ideas and suggestions, what does that teach the children about how they treat their spouses when they marry? What does such negative communication by the husband teach the children about the worth of a woman? Children are observant and quick to understand the lesson parents teach—the good, the bad, and the ugly. Parents do not have to be perfect. Where mistakes are made, parents have an excellent opportunity to teach how to eat humble pie, apologize, and change negative behaviors. Keeping your eyes on the prize also means that both parents are there physically and emotionally for each other and their children. Time with the family needs to be the top priority for every mother and father—it's time to move from hedonism to collectivism, when one marries and has children, otherwise nothing will work right in the marriage or the family.

Now let's look at several negative family traits, the old baggage that carries on wholly or in bits and pieces from generation to generation. Children can learn from the negative lessons of parents exhibiting "crazy" behaviors and from parents exhibiting "healthy" behaviors, but as negative lessons retards a child's development, we need to give this darker side closer scrutiny.

Magical Thinking

"Thomas at this time is the picture of health, and so many strangers remark about it. Certainly makes me happy, because I certainly do everything to make this so and we're so proud of him." (1/6/41)

"P.S., a stranger predicted Thomas would be a Criminal Lawyer or an Ambassador...Hot dog." (1/6/41)

"Nearly every one who sees Thomas predicts he'll be a football player. He certainly is a mischievous rascal and keeps us on our toes." (6/17/1941)

Like Blanche Dubois, who always relied on the kindness of strangers, Blanche Greenstone relied on the compliments of strangers. (*Tennessee William's A streetcar Named Desire*) Blanche's fallacious thinking that she had caused her son's good health, intelligence, and robust nature, which strangers had found so remarkable, meant that she was a remarkable mother too. But as Thomas went through difficult stages of growth and development that caused strangers to shake their heads and wonder what the mother had done wrong, Blanche could not accept the judgement of strangers. I've done the best I could, she thought. It's just that the kid is turning out sour on his own accord, no matter what I do. This line of fallacy eventually led her to wash her hands of the whole situation on July 9, 1943, when Thomas was three years and seven months old:

"Thomas I'm writing all of this down, so that when you have children of your own, you will understand, I hope. No matter how much worry and trouble you have given us, we wouldn't give you up for all the gold in the world. Only because we love you more than anything else in the world, but you sure are a character and maybe some day you will be a great person."

There was nothing she could do to save her "little darling" from a life of terminal buffoonery. Later there was no joy in Mudville, as the mighty "darling" had struck out at the start of the first year of school, when he was six years and twenty-four days old.

> "We are having a terrible time with Thomas at school…At home, he does very well with everything at present things look bad for promotion to the second grade."

Parents obsessed with the performances of their children in public situations often place extreme pressures on themselves, which can lead them into the dark canyons of depression or worse should their children turn out "wrong" or cause a scene in public. Blanche was not the exception to this rule.

Blanche's thinking was not only magical, but was based on false premises. First, Blanche was not the cause of Thomas's good health, striking personality, or robust nature; these were matters of temperament and his pattern of growth and development. But Blanche was a responsible mother, giving Thomas love and attending to his health needs. Blanche did not understand the fine line distinction between the two concepts. Second, Thomas's "bad behaviors" were a normal part of Thomas traveling through various stages and ages of development. Blanche was right; she wasn't responsible for Thomas's behavior. But, not for the reasons (she was the cause) she thought. Blanche was ignorant of the dynamics of child growth and development; so she tried to correct Thomas's "bad behaviors" by administering corporal punishment. Wrong!

The irony of Blanche wanting to give up and throw in the towel when Thomas was young was, in fact, what Thomas needed to continue his growth and development, as nature intended. Blanche's criticisms and harsh punishments to "correct" Thomas's willful disobedience, which were for the most part age-appropriate behaviors, were doomed on two counts. She tried to correct the course of nature by force; and she underestimated Thomas's persistence and nature to fight rather than submit to force and punishment. Blanche couldn't simply throw in the towel on Thomas and discontinued the use of force to correct her problem child. She only threw in the towel to cut her failure as a mother, but she continued the use of verbal and physical abuse with Thomas.

<u>Negative Lesson Learned by Thomas</u>: Everything done is for your own good; and when things go wrong, it's your fault.

Great Expectations: All About Living My Fantasies

"[Thomas] has a very striking personality." "Nearly every one…predicts he'll be a football player…" "a Criminal Lawyer…an Ambassador…Hot dog!" "…and maybe some day [he] will be a great person." "…he is very intelligent…able to learn without much effort." "…he still has the personality and plenty of fortitude…" (1941-1945)

Someone once said expect nothing and you won't be disappointed. This is a true statement, but a tad bit pessimistic. From a more positive and realistic perspective, while we should expect our children to do the best they can in key situations, we should never expect our children to make up for our failings. Otherwise, the twisted thinking on this subject goes like this: "I always wanted to be a great person; Thomas will be that great person." Blanche always wanted to take dancing lessons, but after three months of tap dancing lessons he didn't turn into Fred Astaire. Blanche fell in love with the dashing, swashbuckling men on the silver screen. Recall that movies greatly swayed the public and that movies were the place to go. In Frank Capra's romantic comedy, "It Happened One Night", Clark Gable and Claudette Colbert stared in one blockbuster of a film. During one risqué (for the times) scene, Clark Gable took off his shirt and revealed that he was not wearing an undershirt. According to Robert Osborne (Host of Turner Classic Movies, 12/9/03) undershirt sales plummeted worldwide and never recovered. As the head usherette at the Stage Theater in Martinez, Blanche lived the movies day-in and day-out. And evidently Blanche tried to live out her movie fantasies by dressing Thomas in the finest clothes, combing his hair perfectly, and enjoyed his "striking personality". But, Thomas always came home looking disheveled with his hair mussed up, clothes dirty, and his shoes scuffed up.[s, dd] Thomas had started out neat, not like his father, but Thomas too did not turn into the show piece Blanche needed to live her life's fantasies. Thomas was a disappointment despite all of Blanche's criticism, ridicule, yelling, screaming, and lickings.

<u>Negative Lesson Learned By Thomas</u>: I'm responsible for living up to the expectations of others and for making others happy.

Perfectionism and the Blame Game

"Day-in-day-out, year-in-year-out, same old story…and he fights all of us, but boy is he good with his alibis and excuses, and he has plenty of them. He is now in the 8th grade and we're all still after him to study." (March 20, 1953)

Our example of perfectionism centers on Thomas's refusal to study and complete his class and homework assignments; it is but one scenario played in the blame game, which is played by children ages two to one hundred twenty. Webster's World Dictionary defines blame as the act of placing responsibility for an error or fault on someone or something.[45] One player's role is to assign blame and stay perfect. The opposing player's role is to deny blame and stay perfect. Like a computer's monotone digital voice response to error, Thomas has employed the strategy of responding, "It's not my fault," to all accusations of blame. By the eighth grade, Thomas, considered a "bad egg" by Blanche, has almost twelve years experience saying, "It's not my fault" in an infinite variety of ways to all who attempt to cast blame upon him. Evidently, Thomas is winning the blame game, as his opposition is frustrated and his mother and "all the King's horses and all the King's men [can't] put [the cracked and flawed] Humpty Dumpty together again."[46]

According to *Our Baby Book,* blaming Thomas for his "cracked and flawed" behavior is traceable back to when he was stripping himself of all clothing and throwing his clothes out of a second story window at one and one-half years of age. (4/14/41)

After repeatedly being blamed, got-after, and swatted for his bad behaviors, Thomas learned how to play the blame game at an early age. His strategy was to deny any responsibility whatsoever for anything that went wrong. To destroy the opponent's perfection myth and win the blame-game, Thomas had to feign perfection and believe that he did all that his mother and all the king's horses and all the king's men told him to do. Then he would be perfect because perfect eggs have no cracks and therefore have no fault, there is nothing broken to be put together again. Mother and everyone else can't win the blame-game, where there is no admission of fault. The irony is that both sides clearly see their opponent's fault, as someone once said, "He who has no fault is all fault."

When Thomas started public high school, the blame game lost its luster—no blame; no game. The blame game further lost its glitter, when Thomas was in college—no blame, no game. Thomas's first years in the workplace were collegial and positive; and no one played the blame game—no blame, no game. But, once Thomas moved into upper management, the name of the game was blame—a game he could play well. This time there were winners and losers, depending on whom had the power and who could effectively discredit his opponent.

Negative Lesson Learned by Thomas: Deny everything; and place the blame on others. (The sole exception to this rule is when your golf game turns sour, you may blame anyone from the grounds keepers to innocent bystanders.)

Family Secrets

Every family has a couple of skeletons hanging in their closet. The Greenstone family had two classic beauties—one from each side of the family tree.

Skeleton Number One

In the 1940's children were to be seen and not heard. No one could shut Thomas up for long without cutting him into little pieces and flushing him down the toilet. Blanche presents the reader with a clear picture of how she felt as a mother who has lost complete control of her child. At three years of age Thomas's every outrageous act is another dagger that pierces Blanche's heart.

> "...I'm at my wits end." (7/9/43) "What a life I'm commencing to turn gray." (7/9/43) "Thomas is a little demon." (8/43)

On the evening of July 9, 1943 the spirit of a bewildered and frustrated mother at rope's end penned the following account of child abuse without batting an eye.

> "I was washing clothes on the roof. He did the same thing again. I was frantic. When he finally came upstairs again I gave him a terrible licking with a coat hanger that night when he went to bed his legs were black and blue and I was just sick all over. He just had shorts on at the time of the licking and that must have been the reason for the marks cause heaven only knows he has had several good ones. If this licking would of stopped him from running away it would have been worth it but half an hour later he repeats the same stunt. So I swear this will be my last licking but I'm at an end because he absolutely will not mind me. (7/9/43)

Of course the trail of evidence regarding Thomas's physical abusive treatment runs back to Thomas being swatted for biting (1/28/41) and runs forward through March 20, 1953, when Blanche broke a broom handle hitting Thomas in a fit of rage.

The trail of Thomas's sadistic behaviors over the years attests to his internal rage. Thomas has quite a temper (10/29/41). He fights at Sunday school. (7/9/43) Sets ants on fire. (January 1945) Throws match boxes full of insects into the street so cars can run over them. (January 1945) Thomas is bossy and orders his friends around. (2/22/47) Sells newspapers at the racetrack and hustles the crowd. (1947) He is foul-mouthed at the drop of a hat. (10/12/48, 10/26/48, 10/

9/49, Summer of 1952) He deliberately hurts other kids. (6/11/48) Swears and punches Bill and starts grass fire after hacking frogs to death. (6/11/48) Thomas sets fires around the house and neighborhood. (3/6/50) He roams the streets looking for a fight, not caring if he lives or dies. (12/52) Thomas is suspended from the YMCA for shooting a bobby pin through a kid's lip because he was bothering him. (10/9/50) He bites Eddie through the skin. (3/51) Shoplifts every chance he gets. (4/53) He brutalizes weak staff members at Camp Loma Mar. (4/25/55)

At times Thomas would find himself slapped across the face by his mother and an occasional teacher because he had a smile on his face when they scolded him. He remembers his abusers saying, "Take that smile off your face; or I'll take it off for you." He was never aware that he was smiling; and he certainly didn't want another smack! Many years latter, Dr. Greenstone read an article in a professional journal about "sadistic exhilaration". Evidently, some children smile when abused because at a subconscious level they find pleasure in by having enraged the adult abusing them.

In the 1940's and 1950's, corporal punishment was not prohibited by law and was practiced in most families. Many readers will say after finishing this section, "That was mild compared to what I got as a kid; and it never hurt me." But, many that voice this opinion often engage in road rage and/or have problems that affect their relationships with their wives, children, bosses, and/or colleagues.

Today, a perceived criticism, blame statement, or disrespectful act still hurts and can get a rise out of Dr. Greenstone. Physical abuse is no longer at issue these days, but Greenstone remains ever vigilant in this regard.

<u>Negative Lesson Learned by Thomas</u>: I'm responsible for my parents' faults.

Skeleton Number Two

> "Mom always gave gag-gifts to Dad. One was a picture of a yellow-faced man hiccuping with blue bubbles rising in the air. The man was holding a martini glass had a stupefied expression on his face. The picture inscription read, 'Drinking again Sam.'" (10/9/50)

As a young child, Dr. Greenstone recalls watching his father sprawled on his back, asleep (passed-out) in the middle of the living room rug, peeing straight up in the air. Sam's addiction to pain medications and alcohol also eluded mention in *Our Baby Book*. At sixteen years of age or so, while helping his father paint one of the apartments Blanche and Sam owned, Dr. Greenstone remembers peering through the crack between the bathroom door and the wall and seeing his father guzzling down a quart of Royal Gate Gin. The bright sunlight shown through the window and striking the dancing liquid in the bottle, which exploded into thousands of blinding diamond-like slivers and slashes of light. This may explain why Sam was so calm all the time; and often fell asleep in his favorite chair with the newspaper opened on his chest. Sam had bottles of gin and vodka stashed all over the mortuary, never in the apartment.

Toward the end of Sam's life, Dr. Greenstone would get calls in the middle of the night from the jailer at Santa Rita County Jail requesting someone to pick up his father the next day. Although Sam had three DWI's, the jailer knew and liked Sam. Everybody liked Sam; he was a happy drunk.

Dr. Greenstone sent Sam on a three-month cruise around the world. Written instructions were given to the purser to parcel money out to Sam and under no circumstances extend Sam credit. A few months after Sam got back from the cruise he passed away. Two weeks afterwards, Dr. Greenstone received a letter from the cruise ship company informing him that Sam had run up a five thousand, eight hundred and forty-seven dollar bar bill. Greenstone sent a copy of the letter he had given the purser and his attorney's business card to the cruise Ship Company; and that was the last he heard of the bar bill.

Thomas never drank until he was twenty-one and living on his own. And that is when skeleton #2 began to take its toll. Greenstone admits that he could never handle alcohol gracefully, as the second skeleton out of the closet seems to unleash the demons within his breast. Sam was a "happy" drunk, who simply went to sleep after it was all said and done; his son was a "mean" drunk, who became foul-mouthed, aggressive, and at times violent. Father and son were hell bent on the path to self-destruction. Sam made it; Thomas didn't. So far so good as Blanche would say.

Negative Lesson Learned by Thomas: I'm responsible for my parents' faults.

Variable Stars in the Constellation Lyra

Throughout eighty percent of a star's life journey its luminosity varies little. There exists, however, a type of star that varies greatly in brilliance throughout most of its journey, the variable star. Among the variable stars[47] it's the RR type stars in the Lyra Constellation remind us of Thomas's childhood journey. RR stars vary in brilliance every one and one-half to twenty-four hours.[48] Thomas's "striking personality" changed irregularly throughout each day in consonance with perceived threats, verbal abuses, and/or physical punishments. Sometimes dimming, other times raging, the mood of this RR Lyra star was obvious to the naked eye.[49] Blanche, the Brightest star in Thomas's sky, focused on Thomas's hour to hour variations and saw an erratically behaving, willful child, a dimming star. Others in Thomas's life saw the brilliancy of his star, as their approach to the "mischievous rascal" of a star was accepting and friendly. Others saw mostly dazzle, as Thomas tried to avoid and impress them. And some saw a raging star, as they posed a threat to Thomas.

Dimming, sparkling, and raging through childhood, Thomas entered adulthood and the workplace. Described as "volatile", brilliant and down right "dangerous" by some, Thomas earned his way vertically through another organization. Treated as a fellow and colleague, Thomas worked well under a variety of bosses. Verbally attacked by bosses, who were authoritarian, was not a good match. When corporate politics turned vicious, Thomas counter attacked. His counter-attacks were defensive responses, forceful and delivered with extreme prejudice. His strategic strikes were designed to catch his tormentors off guard and to disable their abilities to harm him further. He was a formidable adversary, if pushed to the wall, but would entertain a compromise if hostilities stopped. Otherwise, Thomas was a pleasant, resourceful, hard working, competent worker, who never held a grudge and who genuinely liked friend and foe. The workplace is, after all, a family of sorts; and all Thomas, now Dr. Greenstone, was doing was playing out his Dr. Jekyll and Mr. Hyde personality. "Scary Donut", as his daughter Kim used to say.

An Only Child

Mention the words "only child" and reactions pour forth. "Such spoiled brats." "They never learn to share." "They never think of anyone, but themselves." In 1945, Blanche preferred the phrase, "spoiled-monkey". *Our Baby Book* tells of numerous adults who fawned over Thomas in his early childhood; and the lists of Christmas and Birthday presents Thomas received each year attests to the fact that Thomas did not want for things or attention. The affect all these people and things had on Thomas allowed him to run amuck. Thomas came to expect gifts from people; and those gifts needed to be the gifts he wanted otherwise he would plunge into sadness or fly into a tantrum—a little monster. Dr. Greenstone recalls how, as a child, he would tear through a present's wrapping, toss away the card, and rip into the box, looking for his bone. Did Thomas give any thought to the person who gave the gift? Did he appreciate the special meaning, which may have been part of the gift? Greenstone has no recollection of such thoughts or appreciation's. The toy was the thing; nothing else mattered.

In Thomas's case being an only child retarded his social sensibilities and development. It wouldn't be until 1960 when Thomas was dating his wife to be,

Marie Castellanos, that he was introduced to how families should accept gifts.[ll] The Greenstone and the Castellanos family cultures were very different in this regard. The Castellanos tradition of gift giving has the gift receiver personally acknowledging each gift by words, hugs and kisses, and heart-felt thank-you notes. While Blanche and Sam acknowledged gifts in a similar manner, somehow the tradition broke down with Thomas. Why did the breakdown occur? Dr. Greenstone's best guess has two parts. First, as a child he was indulged and spoiled-rotten. Second, he learned that gift giving was about you, and not about others!

Greenstone remembers that when he was about eight years old, he had saved his money to buy an Osterizer Blender for his mother on her birthday. According to Greenstone's recollection:

> "Mom hit the ceiling like a banshee, swearing at me something fierce."

Blanche was angry because she believed the gift to be about what Thomas wanted rather than what she wanted. Blanche literally threw the gift aside, and figuratively threw the gift back in Thomas's face. She loudly voiced her displeasure with Thomas's selfishness, and vowed that the gift would be returned to the store. After Blanche's emotional outburst, Sam told Blanche that the Osterizer gift idea was his idea, when he and Thomas went shopping for Blanche's birthday present—Oops! It didn't matter, however, Blanche still saw the birthday gift as an unforgivable, selfish act on Thomas's part. To this day, nothing of this nature was ever to found to be in the fiber of the Castellanos family.

Another bonus that came with coupling the Castellano (new blood) and the Greenstone families was that the Castellanos family was an example of a healthy and functioning family. Thomas was attracted to the family that he never had. From Marie's parents[ll] to Marie's three sisters and brother healthy family relationships abounded, as it did in the Guerino family.[oo] There were saints in the Castellanos family! Nena, Marie's mother's sister, lived with and took care of several generations of children, including Marie, Kim and Michael. She lived to be 101, passing away in 2001. And there is Connie Castellanos, a saint if there ever was one, who is Kim's Godmother and Megan's Great Aunt.

Post Script

Blanche was somehow blocked from an understanding of how her verbal and physical abuse fueled Thomas's angry behavior. As a consequence, Blanche plunged into dark despair and continued to protect herself from self-scrutiny, protecting her fragile self and projecting her failures onto her only child. Blanche's bubbly "Boop-Oop-A-Doo" and "Oh, you kid!" personality ran aground on the rugged rocks of limited understandings, poor self-worth, spiritual bankruptcy, obsessive thinking, and the failure of raising an incorrigible child. Her thinking was what Robert Burney calls "stinking thinking", where rigid extremes—good or bad, right or wrong, love it or leave it, one or ten dominates the thinking process. As Blanche's writing reveals there were no gray areas when it came to raising Thomas, only black and white extremes.[50]

As a child faced by seemingly overwhelming adversity, Thomas developed a Swiss cheese morality. When life dealt a somewhat balanced hand of ups and downs, high moral behavior is the rule and Thomas chose to ignore and over-come adversity. But when life threatens one's life, as was the case in Thomas's family and school organizational environments, all bets are off and one's survival instinct takes over—Dr. Jekyll becomes Mr. Hyde.

Blanche lived long enough to see Thomas become an accomplished company executive. At the age of sixty-one, she died of cerebral aneurysms (1968) shortly after seeing her first granddaughter, whom she loved dearly.

Sam's block was more of an alcoholic blur. His thinking worked more like a dimmer switch. When the switch was fully ON, Sam's thinking was brilliant, logical, problem solving orientated, and fully capable of seeing extremes as well the shades of gray. As alcohol consumption increased, Sam's thinking became slow, fuzzy, and blurred. In the OFF position, Sam's thinking was lights out. As his alcoholism took its toll over time, Sam stayed the course to self-destruction.

Sam also died at the age of sixty-one. The cause of death on his death certificate read natural causes. He enjoyed both of his grandchildren, Kim and Michael.

PART IV

RANDOM CHANCE OR THE HAND OF GOD
(The Twelfth Piece)

"Silent as though in evening contemplation weaves the bat under the gathering stars.
Silent as dew, we seek new incarnation, meditate new avatars."
(Miracles, Conrad Aiken, 1889-1973)

"It turns out that an eerie type of chaos can lurk just behind a facade of order—
And yet, deep inside the chaos lurks an even eerier type of order."
(Douglas Hofstadter, Indiana University Professor,
Computer and Cognitive Sciences)

"Out of the night that covers me, black as the pit from pole to pole,
I thank whatever gods may be for my unconquerable soul. In the fell clutch
Of circumstance, I have not winced nor cried aloud; under the bludgeoning
Of chance my head is bloody, but unbowed."
(William Henley, iv. Invictus)

Next time you say "good luck" or may "God be with you" to someone, bear in mind that you are calling on a mystical power that affects everything from a bet on a horse, to the flight of a golf ball, to the beginnings and endgames of our lives. So long as we are on this side of the mortal veil, we may believe, but we will never know beyond a shadow of a doubt and to a moral certainty whether it's God or Chance that affects our lives.[48] Regardless of our beliefs, however, we do know that bazillions of factors are at play in our lives and our universe at any given moment. When we consider that these bazillions factors are energized differently and multi-dimensionally relate to each other in variety of microenviron-

143

ments, our human capacity to understand the complexity of the universe seems dwarfed. I wouldn't go as far as to say that life is a total crapshoot, but I find it difficult to deny the significant role "chance" plays in shaping being and influencing life's journey. Whether one is born into the family of a Beverly Hill's movie star or into an Aboriginal family in the Australian out back is a matter of "chance." And, as the result of such "chance happenings" our thinking, feelings, and lives set us in different directions. Of all the factors that seem to influence our lives (e.g. parents, friends, institutions, the choices we make), "chance" is the dominant factor, larger than education, money, position, personal makeup, politics, etc.

In our discussion of the human life cycle in a nutshell (See above Part III.) the process begins with "Developed from an egg having a unique combination of chromosomes that form a genetic-self." Now we will explore the question: What happened before we developed from an egg into a genetic-self? Whether dropped into existence by random chance, fate, or the Hand of God, the results are analogous to playing Pachinko.[51]

In this sense our live paths resemble the path taken by an 11-millimeter steel ball as it falls through a pachinko game.[52] Now imagine the following hypothetical. You drop into existence through the top hole of the pachinko game. Bouncing in a 20-degree upward fashion on the first steel pin (representing say…born in Oakland, 10/9/39), you strike another steel pin (representing say…having Blanche as your mother), then ricochet downward at six-o'clock, you strike another steel pin (representing say…attending Saint Francis de Sales School…). Next you knock around the other steel pin events in your life until you exit the game. Another person's life events can be mapped in the same fashion with none of life paths being exactly the same. This rather linear life flow analogy becomes more complex when the turbulence we experience in life is examined.

Chaos Theory

"A plume of cigarette smoke rises smoothly from an ashtray, accelerating until it passes a critical velocity and splinters into wild eddies."[53]

This apparently simple, but nonlinear physical happening remains a complete mystery that physicists and mathematicians can't figure out to this day. Here, we are dealing with just a handful of factors: the chemical composition of a cigarette, which is burning in air. Yet this simple turbulence event defies our abilities to predict outcomes. Since the time of Claudius Ptolemy (150 A.D.), scientists have accurately explained stellar events, such as the retrograde motion of planets, and have accurately predicted future positions of heavenly bodies.[54] However, predicting where a molecule of C10H14N2 (nicotine) lodged within a cigarette will wind up in a plume of smoke is an impossible task for science. Mind you, we are dealing only with physical matter. Living matter becomes a much more complex and perplexing issue. Predicting which human zygote will grow up to be a crook, BART-train driver, or President of the United States is, for the same chaotic reason, an impossible task for parents and teachers to predict.

In the early 1990's, I was asked to make a few remarks to a group of scientists at Lawrence Livermore National Laboratory (LLNL) at one of the lab's educational conferences. As I stepped to the podium, it seemed that most of these fellows, particularly physicists, seemed to be looking at me, as if I was some Pre-Columbian Shaman chewing on a coca leaf.[55] What could an educator possibly have to say to these brilliant fellows, who routinely use mathematics, technology, and the laws of physics to routinely launch rockets into space and smart bombs into Baghdad with incredible precision?

I told them a true story about a physicist who taught a lesson on momentum to a group of twenty kindergarten children—a story that seemed to especially delight the biologists in the audience. For about a minute, everything went smoothly in the classroom. Then, like ants let out of a jar, the kids wiggled about and engaged the scientist in a barrage of unrelated conversations and questions. "Teacher, Johnny is touching me." "My grandma gave me this sweater for my birthday." Where's Kathy?" The kindergarten teacher was able to get the ants back into the jar by sounding three notes on the tone blocks (…the old NBC tones we used to hear on the radio). By the end of the lesson the poor fellow was a nervous wreck and awfully frustrated.

The scientist knew his subject and presented the lesson in a logical and entertaining manner. He couldn't believe the unruly nature of the children in this class, although he missed the ease with which the teacher had brought the class to order. He blamed his inability to teach the children on everything from hell to breakfast, but couldn't grasp the problem—a biological turbulence problem, the likes of which he had never before seen.

"Turbulence is a mess of disorder at all scales; small eddies with large ones, unstable in all respects. Turbulence drains energy and creates drag. Turbulence is motion turned random.[56]

In 1963, meteorologist Edward Lorenz created a famous concept now known as the Butterfly Effect, when he asked the question: Does the flap of a butterfly's wings in Brazil set off a tornado in Texas?[57] Weather reporting is an excellent example of the prediction-defying nature of physical science. So much is known about weather, but how accurate will tomorrow's weather forecast be? The return of Haley's comet and the ocean tides are fairly well predictable; why not weather? Lorenz's conclusion was that although the tides, movements of heavenly bodies, and atmospheric events are governed by the same laws of physics, weather is a very much more complicated problem. With weather small events, like small puffs of wind, taken together within a small space, say one cubic inch of air can create large effects or no effect or create incredibly different effects from time-to-time. The kicker is that, while the particulars of weather are unfathomable at some level, weather produces clear and familiar patterns, marine layers, rain cycles, the sound of falling snow, thunderheads, as well as various other cloud formations.

Today, Chaos theory has waned from the view of the public, which was amazed when the theory was popularized in 1989. From Newton to Einstein to the mysterious connections of quantum mechanics, the world in which we live is as uncertain and unpredictable as ever.[74]

As with plumes of smoke and weird quantum entanglements, human behavior seems chaotic, probable, and escapes prediction. But, as a practical matter, such human uncertainty moves generation after generation to the beat of familiar patterns and unified principles. Parents, grandparents, and teachers need to understand and appreciate these recurring patterns and underlying principles to improve our child-raising and teaching practices. We need to read and understand more of life's poetry, and not be distracted by life's chaos.

> "I spied a red-backed spider
> Leaping high, snag and bite
> A dark metalic-blue blowfly
> Then, return upon a garden wall
> Without a missed step or a fall.
> Were two actors
> In ancient play?
> Or, did theses beings
> Have their way?
> And how did I wander by
> To glimpse the spider and the fly?

Pure happenstance,
Most would say.
Sheer luck
Along a garden lane.
But I consider other fare.
There was reason in the air.[58]

PART V

EPILOGUE

"Courage brother! Do not stumble,
Though thy path is dark as night; there's a star
To guide the humble; trust in god, and do the right."
(Norman Macleod, Edinburgh Christian Magazine, January 1857)

"Surrender yourself humbly; then you can be trusted to care for all things.
Love the world as your own self; then you can truly care for all things."
(Lao Tsu, Tao Te Ching, Part 13, 500 B.C.)

Grandparents' hand a mixed bag of learned behavior patterns and genetic dispositions to their children who hand an augmented mixed bag of behaviors and genetics to their children who continue handing off the mixed bags to their progeny. Thus, the mixed bags of the good, the bad, and the ugly continue from generation to generation. Knowing this, we, parents and grandparents, need to closely attend to the behavior patterns we imprint our children lives, as such imprints do affect their lives, often to in unintended ways. The question is what do we need to do for our children and grandchildren to better position them to achieve true fulfillment and happiness? To adequately answer this question, we must understand the nature of timing, chaos, values, and personal renewal, as to us, as parents and grandparents, while we are still active on life's stage.[59]

Timing

Often we think of our parents as being out of step with the times. However, within the context of they're times, Blanche and Sam were good parents. They, in fact, were in step with their times. The problem is, as we look back at their time, we see their flaws because we stand on higher ground, which is built on the advances of education and science. Our parents did the best they possibly could, given their upbringing and circumstances. And, if we were in their places, we can only hope that we could have done as well. Back in Thomas's parent's day smoking, corporal punishments, producing respectful and obedient children, who were to be seen and not heard, were the culturally acceptable expectations of their day. As parents and grandparents looking back at how we were raised, we need to keep these facts in mind, even if our parents abused us or worse! As parents looking back on our parents' flaws and weaknesses, we need to be forgiving or, at least, understanding. As parents, we can only hope that our children, when looking back on their parent's flaws, will be so compassionate and understanding, to be forgiving of our failings.

Patterns of Life

Many choose to view life as hopelessly complex and beyond human understanding. But, our study of the twelve pieces of Thomas's life cycle paints a rosier picture. Those who have lived long enough and have most of their marbles in tact, clearly see that we have had far more control over our lives than first imagined and can correct most of the errors of our youth. This is a piece of old wisdom. Since Adam and Eve became grandparents, the problem has been how to convince our children and our institutional leaders to listen to and follow the wisdom infused in the experience of a lifetime? The problem with older people sharing with younger people and institutions their experiences and accumulative wisdom of a lifetime is threefold. First, the young are caught up in making it on their own, which is exactly what all of us have to do. The young won't be in a position to gain wisdom until they are old. Then, they face the same problem as we do: nobody seems to listen to old people. (Keep in mind that virtually all parents are young!) Second, institutions are supremely complicated and, by their nature, are against the individual. Institutions are filled with young people, who are tired of old people telling them what to do and are filled with old people, who haven't yet stepped back from the rat race to examine their lives and gain wisdom. So, we can cross institutions and the people contained in them off our list as being feckless entities not worth our time to change. Unless, you are a consultant, making big buck off the institutions. Third, considering human nature as it is, most old people discount the validity of the young person's life experience—big mistake, not listening to the wisdom of the young. The "shut-up and list" schools of wisdom, in American society, usually doesn't work. Although, certain branches of Zen and martial arts do have their good points. Chaos! All is lost? No, just the opposite is true. Consider two points. There are, in fact, very wise people of all ages roaming around on earth and we do have more control over the twelve pieces of our lives, discussed in this story, than we think we do.

Factors Beyond Our Control: Piece #1: Determining our genetic-self, including our eye color, temperaments, intelligence, resiliency traits, etc. Piece #2: Controlling our biologically driven stages of growth and development. Piece #3: How our parents were raised and will raise us. Piece #11: Knowing the exact day and time of our demise or of the extinction of our species and universe. Piece #12: Knowing the time and place we will appear on life's stage, whether we will be able to biologically create children, and knowing the exact hand to be dealt to us by God or Fate.

Factors Well in the Grasp of our Control: Piece #3*: How we raise our children. Piece #4: Learning from our own life experiences and the experiences of others. Piece #: What we learn from nature. Piece # 11: Shaping and being shaped by culture and social institutions (Just because I have given up on social institutions doesn't have bearing on your ability to grab an institution or two by the tail and make them cry uncle.) Piece #12: Mate with another genetic-self.

Factors in our Control: Piece #3:* How we choose to treat and influence our children, grandchildren, and great grandchildren. Piece # 8: Thinking, wondering, questioning, tinkering, learning, exercising free will, creating, and destroying. Piece #9: Exercising our abilities to reinvent ourselves at any given moment in life. Piece #12: Whether we choose to believe or not believe in God.

* The repetition of and variations on Piece # 3 reflects Thomas's recently emerged views on the value of family, a value he thought he had embraced, when he was a younger husband and father, but realizes, now, that baggage from own family upbringing and his own unhealthy life decisions had distorted his sense of family values.

While there are some pieces of our lives over which we have no control, we do have a substantial control over the other pieces, which allow us, not only to understand the emerging pattern of chaos in our lives, but, to exercise free choice in determining our direction and improving the quality of our lives. In point of fact, one may build quite a formidable case for believing that the pieces of our lives beyond our control have only negligible impact on our lives

Take, for one example, the genetic inheritance of intelligence. As one of my college professors once said: any child that can find his way to school has sufficient intelligence to succeed. There is more truth in this statement than first comes to eye. Children come into life supremely hardwired to learn; where children run into learning difficulties, it is usually the adults in a family, school system, or social institution that are responsible for learning difficulties. Thank goodness for another genetic mechanism called resiliency (the ability to overcome the odds), which is arguably distributed more or less evenly throughout humanity and is triggered and enhanced by hard times. By virtue of resiliency many children overcome the "learning difficulties" they face in life. Our normal human intelligence works well (although one could argue very well that humanity because of it's intelligence walks on the edge of extinction) to keep us at the top of our food chain. Whenever an individual human emerges on life's stage, he or she does arrive at the furthermost advancement of human progress with sufficient intelligence and resilience to make further advancements. To illustrate, consider the time into which a newborn arrived in 580 B.C., when the cutting edge of physics claimed water to be the basis of all things—a concept not entirely wrong by today's standards and the smallest particle of matter the atom. Compared this time of arrival to the time when Megan (Thomas's grandchild) appeared in 2004 A.D, when the cutting edge of physics says that a length of energy (several hundred billion billion times smaller that an atom in an eleven dimension framework make up the basic fabric of all existence—a concept physicists' refer to as M-Theory. Clearly, both newborns arrived at the peaks of scientific progress that explain their cultures and direct their thinking. Relatively speaking, neither was born into a disadvantaged time, which flew beyond their intellectual capacities. Finally, as for the knowing the time of our demise and the extinction, such matters are highly overrated, if we make use of the time we have and are not driven by questions we can't answer.

As we evaluate the individual patterns of our lives, it is apparent that we are in control of a great many more of the factors that affect our lives than we at first realize—the odds for success are on our side. The swing question is how long will it take us to realize the truth revealed by the patterns emerging from the seeming chaos of our lives. For Dr. Greenstone, it took over sixty years; and he's still working at it. As for the mythological Lucifer, he still doesn't get it or doesn't want to get it. Greenstone's life is now more abundant, full of opportunity—optimism rules his days and nights. For Lucifer, life remains a bit of a drag—pessimism rules supreme.

Enduring Questions

Throughout Thomas's story the author has been dancing around questions of religious beliefs. Does God exist? And, if so, what is our mission in life? Our examination of these questions is important in that the answers strike at the heart of Piece #12, which is beyond our mortal understanding. The topic can't be easily brushed away with a flick of the hand and saying so what! Why? Those who deny God or deny that some power beyond exists us, to which we are accountable, usually end up hollow-feeling, depressed, or in constant manic denial to sustain their Non-Belief. The life of one of the most incredibly brilliant men in history, who certainly explored the mind's recesses, testifies to this point. "Freud's arguments were militantly hostile to God's existence. Yet his logic predicted ambivalence. Reflecting this ambivalence, he himself remained preoccupied throughout his life with the question of God's existence. He was in deep preoccupied with the 'infantile' 'fairy tale' of God's existence." [*The Questions of God* by *Dr. Armand Nicholi, Jr., Associate Clinical Professor of Psychiatry, Harvard University, p. 50 (2002)]* The truth is that we must hold ourselves accountable to some hirer power to realize our individual human potentials and to successfully develop the human potentials of those entrusted to us within our families.

God Exists[60]

"Man lives not by material bread alone." (Hinduism)

"Man shall not live by bread alone, but by every word of God." (Christianity)

"Make divine knowledge thy food." (Sikhism)

"Man doth not live by bread alone, but by every word that proceedeth out of the mouth of the Lord." (Judaism)

Our mission, therefore, is to seek God and love one another.[61]

"Oh Great Spirit, grant that I may never find fault with my neighbor until I have walked the trail of life in his moccasins." *(Cherokee Prayer, unknown author)*

"One going to take a pointed stick to pinch a baby bird should first try it on himself to feel how it hurts." *(Yoruba Proverb, author unknown)*

"Thou shalt love thy neighbor as thyself." (Judaism)

"Full of love for all things in the world, practicing virtue in order to benefit others, this man alone is happy." (Buddhism)

"A man obtains a proper rule of action by looking on his neighbor as himself. (Hinduism)

"A new commandment I give you, That you love one another; even as I have loved you…By this all men will know that you are my disciples, if you have love for one another." (Christianity)

Nature Exists

"The Tao that can be told is not the eternal Tao. The name that can be named is not the eternal name. The nameless is the beginning of heaven and earth. The named is the mother of ten thousand things. Ever desireless, one can see the mystery. Ever desiring, one can see the manifestations. These two spring from the same source but differ in name; this appears as darkness. Darkness within darkness. The gate to all mystery."[62]

Our mission, therefore, is to seek nature and follow its way.

"The greatest Virtue is to follow Tao and Tao alone. The Tao is elusive and intangible. Oh, it is intangible and elusive, and yet within is image. Oh, it is elusive and intangible, and yet within is form. Oh, it is dim and dark, and yet within is essence. This essence is very real and therein lies faith. From the very beginning until now its name has never been forgotten. Thus I perceive the creation. How do I know the ways of creation" Because of this."[63]

"Why is the sea king of a hundred streams? Because it lies below them. Therefore it is the king of a hundred streams. If the sage would guide the people, he must serve with humility. If he would lead them, he must follow behind. In this way when the sage rules, the people will not feel oppressed; When he stands before them, they will not be harmed. The whole world will support him and will not tire of him. Because he does not compete, he does not meet competition."[64]

God doesn't exist. What is our mission in life?

Sam was an atheist, but not irreligious. Sam was not indifferent or hostile to religion. He did not scoff at funeral services or at the beliefs of others. Sam believed his purpose in life was to serve his community, meeting the needs of people in grief—his mission on earth was humanistic.

Literature is chock-full of atheistic writers, telling of their struggles with the God questions and of their conclusions after all is said and done. One such author is Albert Camus, who was born in 1913 and was awarded the Nobel Prize for Literature in 1957, a few years before his death in a car accident on January 4,

1960. He was an author who did not believe in God. His lead characters often wrestled with problems of faith and belief. In his novel, *The Plague*, Camus main character (Dr. Bernard Rieux) comes to realization that "those whose desires are limited to man and his humble yet formidable love, should enter, if only now and then, into their reward."[65] Equally, many patriarchs of Christianity (e.g., St. Peter, St. Thomas, St. Jerome, St. Augustine) have struggled with their beliefs and faith and have come to the same conclusion as Camus. "For now we see through a glass, darkly; but then face to face: now I know in part; but then shall I know even as also I am known. And now abideth faith, hope, and charity, these three; but the greatest of these is charity [love]."[66]

In Conrad's book, *The Heart of Darkness*, the main character, Mr. Kurtz, starts up the Congo River with the noble intention of making every company station along the Congo River a beacon light, signaling a better way of life for the "savages". But, alone and unchecked, Kurtz gives in to his basic nature, allowing the "savages" to be worshipped him as their god. Responding to Marlow's questions, the "harlequin" man describes Kurtz:

> "You don't talk with Mr. Kurtz?" I said. "You don't talk with that man—you listen to him."[67] "We talked of everything...." "I forgot there was such a thing as sleep..." He made me see things"[68]

> "He could be very terrible. You can't judge Mr. Kurtz as you would an ordinary man. No, no, no! Now—just to give you an idea—I don't mind telling you, he wanted to shoot me too one day-but I don't judge him."[69]

> "In a hurried, indistinct voice [the harlequin man] began to assure me he had not dared to take these—say, symbols down.[70] He was not afraid of the natives; they would not stir till Mr. Kurtz gave the word. His ascendancy was extraordinary. The camps of these people surrounded the place, and the chief came every day to see him. They would crawl..."[71]

The punch line to the ending of Conrad's novel comes when Kurtz realizes the "horror" of his actions and how far he had fallen from his noble aims. Pierced by a native's spear, Kurtz dies in this state of torment. Conrad played out the common religious theme that when mortals stray from the will of God, become untied from morale principles, terrible things happen.

Philosophy

"What thou avoidest suffering thyself seek not to impose on others" (*Encheiridion, Epictetus, 100 A.D.*)

"What stirs your anger when done to you by others, that do not to others." [*Advice to Nicocles*, Socrates (b. 469 B.C.)]

"Treat your inferiors as you would be treated by your superiors" (*Epistle 47:11, Seneca, Rome, 1st century A.D.*)

"May I do to others as I would that they should do unto me." (*Plato, 4th century B.C.*)

Evolution

"I fully subscribed to the judgments of those writers who maintain that of all the differences between man and the lower animals, the moral sense or conscience is by far more the most important…It is the most noble of all the attributes of man, leading him without a moment's hesitation to risk his life for that of a fellow-creature; or after due deliberation, impelled simply by the deep feeling of right or duty, to sacrifice it in some great cause…The following proposition seems to me in a high degree probable—namely, that any animal whatever, endowed with wellmarked social instincts, the parental and filial affections being here included, would inevitably acquire a moral conscience." (*Charles Darwin, The Descent of Man, 1871*)

In Closing

Christians, religious believers of all stripes, naturalists, atheists, philosophers, evolutionists, and all mixtures of the above highly regard the sanctity of human life, recognize the human predisposition to love one another, and acknowledge the responsibility we have to manage our ourselves and our environments in positive and constructive ways. Each belief, whether examined through introspection and reason alone or accepted purely by faith hold the individual accountable to the ways of God, nature, and/or humanity, which are all mysteries—far larger than any human being. And, where do we first learn about God, the sanctity of human life, and our life's mission? You've got it! We learn these truths at our mother's knee[kk] and wrapped in our father's arms,[nn] which is the prime mission of society's first institution, the family. So, it's to our children, grandchildren, and great grandchildren, those precious little gems that God and fate entrusts to us and to whom we owe the duty to teach how to seek God, to love of life, love self, and to love of others.

And, if we faithfully and positively carry out the prime mission, as parents and teachers, community and church leaders, extending ourselves into society at large, as good family members and strangers, we will receive all of God and fate's blessings. We will experience the exhilaration of self-renewal by experiencing through a child's innocence, wonder, and eagerness to learn that shines brightly in their trusting eyes.[mm]

"At the same time came the disciples unto Jesus, saying,
Who is the greatest in the kingdom of heaven?
And Jesus called a little child unto him,
And set him in the midst of them.
And said, "Verily I say unto you,
Except ye be converted, and
Become as little children,
Ye shall not enter into
The kingdom of heaven."[72]

He who is filled with Virtue is like a newborn child.
Wasps and serpents will not sting him;
Wild beasts will not pounce upon him;
He will not be attacked by birds of prey.
His bones are soft, his muscles weak,
But his grip is firm.
He has not experienced the union of
Man and woman, but is whole.
His manhood is strong.
He screams all day without becoming horse.
This is perfect harmony.[73]

Marie and Thomas's granddaughter Megan is fast approaching six months of age and is starting to eat rice cereal.[mm] With every mouthful of cereal she teachers, as all children do, her parents, grandparents, Godparents, and great aunt learning and wondering, as do all children. In turn, her parent[oo], grandparents[ll], supporting cast[ii], and the others that she will only see and know through pictures and family stories,[a, aa, b, c, ll] are keenly aware of the critical importance of the small window of time in every child's life, called early childhood. And, this family is giving her all the love and all of the necessities (and then some) to position her well in life. The first part of the marathon is on. Megan's personality is unfolding rapidly. Soon, she will demand her rightful place in society, as a member of the emerging new generation, continuing the human cycle life.

Early in our story, a question was posed: How does a family that is heading toward self-destruction and extinction change course? The answer given was that new blood and healthy behaviors needed to be introduced into the family to eliminate or at least mitigate disastrous results of past generations. For a few grandparents, who live long enough to learn from their mistakes, have the potential to positively impact the lives of their grandchildren and their children, it is possible to exorcise old family demons, cleanse old blood, and change unhealthy behaviors.

Marie and Thomas, continually thank their lucky stars for the second chance to make a positive first impression on Megan's life and to transform the quality of their relationship with their daughter, Kim and son, Michael. And, as for Megan, she could not have picked better parents than Kim and Jason[oo] or a better supporting cast (Uncle-Godfather Michael, Cousin-Godmother Diane, Uncle Ben, Great Aunt Connie, Grandma Marie, and Grandpa Thomas) to accompany through childhood and into adulthood. Rumor has it that the Adam's family constellation will undergo yet another reconfiguration in February 2005; and family lessons learned will be applied to the raising of another human being—the beat goes on promise filled.

"So far, so good" as Blanche would say.

FAMILY ALBUM—as seen from the perspective of Thomas, as a child or an adult):

a. Grandma (Margaret E. Hurst) and Grandpa (Phillip Matthew Greenstone) with Dad.

b.   Grandma Freitas in Martinez (Mary Valladao) and Grandpa Joe (Joe Freitas, Jr.) at their 50th Wedding Anniversary in 1956. Left to right children: Fred, Blanche, and Joe.

c.   Mom in 1927—not bad!

d. Dad's family and friends at the Long Beach Pier in Southern California around 1916. From smallest to largest, Uncle Kenny, Dad, Aunt sissy, I don't know the next three people, Dad's Auntie Esther, Grandpa Philip, and I don't know that guy.

e. When things got financially tough, the family always could deliver icein Long Beach, California—the year of the S.F. earthquake (1909)

f.   Grandpa Phillip (right) and a friend delivering ice. (1909)

g.   Dad was a cowboy, riding the sidewalks of Long Beach to Signal Hill. (1915)

h.   Here's Dad "stumping" for votes under the Long Beach Pier. (1914)

i.   Mom is the Holy Ghost Princess on the right, holding the scepter. Looks like the City of Martinez—home of the original martini—took the festival seriously. (1920)

j.   Just Pals! A picture of Mom (middle) and a couple of friends posing for the camera on the running board of one of their boy friend's convertible. (1926)

k.   Here's Mom and dad on June 14, 1937. Don't ask how I know.

l. Here's Dad with "Dickie" and "Lady" at Grandma's house, when I was just a twinkle in Dad's eye. (April 10, 1938)

m. Mom and me on the running board of our 1937 Plymouth. (January 29, 1940)

n.   Here's Mom and me in the great outdoors. (6/1/40)

o.   Virgil and Mary Caporgno, my godparents, whooping it up in Tijuana, Mexico. (September 6, 1940)

p.   Teddy Bear, Danny Cameron and me—we were inseparable. (March, 1940)

q.   My parents got a kick watching me grab for car bumpers, steps, bushes—anything I could get my hands on to pull myself up and start walking. (September 12, 1940)

r. Loose! They've unsnapped the leash from my harness and I'm free at last; ensure my Mother's worst fears, I take off away from the crowd. (January 11, 1941)

s. Here I am—Old Rough and Ready—I'm standing in the kitchen. Behind me is the food preparation table, under which I stuffed my Uncle Fred, play-fighting in 1956. (March, 1942)

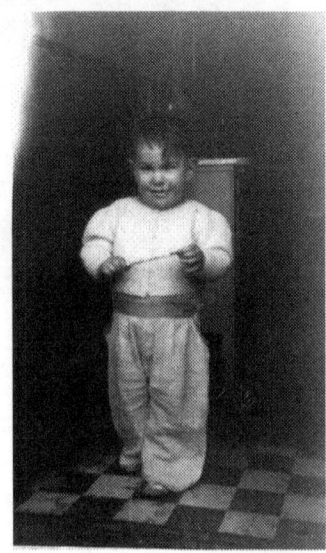

t. My friend Paddy and me playing in the snow at Rainbow Tavern. (April 18, 1942)

u. Here's Dad and me going for a trip in the great outdoors. (1942)

v. Here I am running around on the mortuary roof, while Mom's hanging clothes. One learns lessons rather fast up here. You only brush against the tin sheet metal topped vents (look over my right shoulder) one time in to slice open your leg. (October 1941)

w. My favorite cousin, Steve, and I sitting on the back step of the mortuary, supporting the War effort. (April 9, 1944)

x. Robert Caporgno and I with his dog, "Blackie" in the baby buggy (1944)

y. Here I am leaning against the Flower Wagon, an old hearse, where I used to go when playing hide-and-seek. Robert and I would ride in the back to help our Dads unload flowers. at the cemetery. (1948)

z.   The great outdoors, freedom to run and be free. Maybe Dad's "tallywacker"
     comment was right! (1946)

aa. Aunt Sissy, Dad's older sister, was always nice to me. It was too bad that she
     married Jackass Bill. Opposites do attract, they say. (October, 1943)

bb. Almost every picture shows Dad laughing and smiling when he was with me. He sure loved me. Dad looks like he's porking up a bit and I'm not far behind—there was plenty of food on the table at our house. And, by the way, there's the classic red Radio Wagon—a present from my godparents. (1941)

cc. Here I am riding on my cousin's horse down on the dairy farm in Kern County, California. (June 2, 1943)

June 2, 1943
Taylor at Kerman, Cal.

dd. Percy and Henry Lampkins are my best kindergarten friends. Mom sent me to St. Francis the next year, as she did not like the public school element! (September, 1944)

ee. Oakland Y-camp Ragger emblem: Circle of Friendship, Four-square Way of Life; the Trinity Triangle; and the symbol of Jesus Christ—all dedicated to Life-long Christian Service to children and youth. (1952)

ff.   Standing at the crossing of Telegraph and Broadway and looking down Telegraph, I can see two places that occupied a great deal of time and enjoyment in my life: the Fox Oakland Theater (near left) and the YMCA (next large building on the left with a flag pole on top). And, in the background, the Berkeley hills. (2004)

gg. Here's a page out of *Our Baby Book*—all cutesy and like. Mother had beautiful handwriting and a flair for writing. The sample tells about a great time Mom and I had together on my birthday—one of the last bright days before my world caved in. (1941)

hh. First Grade Drawing on the topic of what my Dad does for a living. Dad's working on a cadaver for the funeral and off to the church. The red thing (Sorry the picture is not in color) above the chest of the body is the embalming fluid, in those days, was fed into and through the body by gravity. (March 6, 1946)

ii. Megan's Baptisms: (left to right) Godmother and 2nd Cousin Diane Aranda, Mother Kim Adams, Megan Adams, Father Jason Adams, and Godfather and Uncle Michael. Either Great Aunt Connie or Uncle Ben took the picture with Grandma Marie watching. Where's Grandpa Thomas? He and Jerry Guerino are in another room, discussing a picture of Christ, which was hung on the wall. Grandpa is an independent soul, who often wanders around away from the crowd, even when the crowd is his own family. Oh, I forgot to mention that Uncle Michael hand made Megan's baptismal dress. (10/26/03)

jj.   Megan was a happy, happy Bumblebee for Halloween. Held in the air by Grandpa Thomas, Megan focuses in on a rose flower, being held by Grandma Marie. (October 31, 2003)

kk.   Kim and Megan, the Sierran star, in the Sierra's looking for a Christmas tree. Mom is a flight nurse at Stanford Hospital; and the hillside is reminiscent of a Reach helicopter crash (not a Stanford helicopter), which killed two nurses and a pilot with whom Kim had flown just a few months ago. Mom is in a dangerous business. (December 2004)

ll. Marie and Thomas with their parents shortly after their wedding reception
     at the Edgewater Inn. From left to right Nicanor Castellanos, Rosario Cas-
     tellanos, Marie Greenstone, Thomas Greenstone, Blanche Greenstone (Frei-
     tas), and Sam Greenstone. My father-in-law's (photo left) life is another
     great family story. In 1924, he left Mexico, worked in Chicago, and, when
     he had enough money, relocated his family in Oakland, California in 1945.
     His children all married and raised families; and all of the Nicanor and Rosa-
     rio's grandchildren are productive and have make their marks in life with
     seven of ten grandchildren graduating from universities. (August 23, 1963)

mm.Fed by Dad Jason in Grandma Marie's arms, Megan experiencing her first spoonful of rice. Just a side note: Don't you think Megan looks like me? Genetics is a scary thing at times. (November, 2004)

nn. Jason and Megan in the snow, looking for Christmas trees—almost lost the both of them, when Jason fell (the athlete, high school P.E. teacher, and football coach) slid down a hill with Megan hanging under him in the björn, like a gondola at Squaw Valley. As you can tell from Megan's expression, she loves everything about the outdoors. (December 2004)

oo. Jerry Guerino and the Boretto Municipio clerk, who found documents verifying that Jerry' grandparents (to be) were married in Boretto, Reggio Emilia Province in the central part of the Po River Valley, Italy. The Guerinos migrated to the United States in 1908. (May 2004)

ENDNOTES

1. Durant, John and Alice. <u>Pictorial History of American Presidents</u>. New York: A.S. Barns and Co. pp. 211 and 304 (1955).

   In the 1904 Presidential Election, Roosevelt, a Republican, ran against Democratic candidate Alton B. Parker. The results of the election were reported as follows: (p. 304)

Candidates	Popular Vote	Electorial Vote
Theodore Roosevelt	7, 628, 834	336
Alton B. Parker	5, 084, 491	140

2. <u>The RFK Assassination</u>. (<u>http://homepages.tcp.co.uk/</u>"dlewis/) Monolith Internet Services International, p. 1 (2003).

3. Durant, John and Alice (1955): p. 245.

4. Miller, Alice. <u>For Your Own Good: Hidden cruelty in child rearing and the roots of violence</u>. New York: Farrar, Straus, and Giroux, p. 3 (1990).

5. There are elements beyond our control that influence the course of our lives. Consequently, one of the presumptions underlying our story is that random chance; chaos or Divine Providence (call it what you will) is the most dominant, ever present force, which affects all life. Throughout our story the reader may have seen the omnipresent hand of Divine Providence or of fortune at work in the life and times of Dr. Greenstone. Again, there is no attempt to argue the merits of religion over random chance or vise versa. There is only the desire to acknowledge the role that either or both of these perspectives have on our views of life.

   Divine Providence: From this perspective God exists and is the good force behind all creation. His Word and His Guidance are what we seek to live as we were meant to live on earth and in the afterlife. This belief sets in motion a variety of views about reality, morality and proper behavior.

Random Chance/Chaos: From this perspective God may or may not exist and Random Chance and Chaos is the force behind all creation. Using our senses and intellect we seek what all creation is about and live the best we can in accordance with the principles of creation. This belief sets in motion a variety of views about reality, morality and proper behavior.

However, the bottom line from both perspectives is that something beyond our understanding profoundly influences our lives. This awareness allows us to learn, understand life, change our behaviors, and gives us the capacity to positively affect ourselves and future generations, starting with our children, grandchildren, great-grandchildren, so forth and so on into society and the world.

6. By using all of the known information about our early childhood experience we can reconstruct a reasonably accurate portrait of our self as a child and youth. While it may be argued that because of the dubious nature of our recollections of our early life and the unknown nature of the forces that affect our lives, it is impossible to know and link the factors of early life affect our maturation and present persona. I would submit to you that while there is some truth in this argument, there is more truth that predictable patterns emerge from of chaos just as clearly as one can see the hand of God working in their life. Consequently, piecing together the puzzle of our youth from the elements and forces discussed and linking our known life events to our present does give us a reliable picture of ourselves and does give us the power to recreate our lives at any given time. And, as with the first presumption, this allows us to learn, understand life, change our behaviors, and gives us the capacity to positively affect ourselves and future generations, starting with our children, grandchildren, great-grandchildren, so forth and so on into society and the world.

7. Stern, Daniel. The Interpersonal World of the Infant: A View from Psychoanalysis and Developmental Psychology. Basic Books a Member of the Perseus Books Group, pp. 3-4 (2000).

8. Neufeldt, V. and Guralnic, D., Editors. Webster's New World Dictionary of American English (3rd College Edition). New York: Prentice-Hall, p. 1377 (1994).

9. Thomas, Alexander and Chess, Stella. <u>Temperament and Development</u>. Brunner/Mazel, INC. 19 Union Square West, New York, N.Y. 10003, pp. 22-23 (1977).

10. Thomas and Chess (1977): pp. 20-22.

The nine categories of temperament created by Thomas and Chess are as follows:

(1. <u>Activity Level</u>: the motor component present in a given child's functioning and the diurnal proportion of active and inactive periods. Protocol data on motility during bathing, eating, playing, dressing and handling, as well as information concerning the sleep-wake cycle, reaching, crawling and walking, are used in scoring this category.

(2. <u>Rhythmicity</u> (Regularity): the predictability and/or predictability in time of any function. It can be analyzed in relation to the sleep-wake cycle, hunger, feeding pattern and elimination schedule.

(3. <u>Approach or Withdrawal</u>: the nature of the initial response to a new stimulus, be it a new food, new toy or new person. Approach responses are positive, whether displayed by mood expression (smiling, verbalizations, etc.) or motor activity (swallowing a new food, reaching for a new toy, active play, etc.). Withdrawal reactions are negative, whether displayed by mood expression (crying, fussing, grimacing, verbalizations, etc.) or motor activity (moving away, spitting new food out, pushing new toy away, etc.).

(4. <u>Adaptability</u>: responses to new or altered situations. One is not concerned with the nature of the initial response, but with the ease with which they are modified in desired directions.

(5. <u>Threshold of Responsiveness</u>: the intensity level of stimulation that is necessary to evoke a discernable response, irrespective of the specific form that the response may take, or the sensory modality affected. The behaviors utilized are those concerning reactions to sensory stimuli, environmental objects, and social contacts.

(6. <u>Intensity of Reaction</u>: the energy level of response, irrespective of its quality or direction.

(7. <u>Quality of Mood</u>: The amount of pleasant, joyful and friendly behavior, as contrasted with unpleasant, crying and unfriendly behavior.

Distractibility: the effectiveness of extraneous environmental stimuli in interfering with or in altering the direction of the ongoing behavior.

(9a. Persistence: the continuation of an activity in the face of obstacles to the maintenance of the activity direction.

(9b. Attention Span: the length of time a particular activity is pursued by the child.

Thomas and Chess scored each temperament category on a three-point scale, in this way:

1. Activity Level: High—Medium—Low
2. Rhythmicity: Regular—Variable—Irregular
3. Approach/Withdrawal: Approach—Variable—Withdrawal
4. Adaptability: Adaptive—Variable—Nonadaptive
5. Response Threshold: High—Medium—Low
6. Reaction Intensity: Positive—Variable—Negative
7. Quality of Mood: Positive—Variable—Negative
8. Distractibility: Yes—Variable—No
9a. Persistence: Yes—Variable—No
9b. Attention Span: Yes—Variable—No

11. Thomas and Chess (1977): pp. 18-19.

The New York Longitudinal Study (NYLS) focused on a sample of 141 children, who were selected 1956 and 1961. The initial sample was selected from middle to upper-middle class families. Forty percent of the mothers and sixty percent of the fathers had advanced college degrees with less than ten percent having no college. Seventy-eight percent of the parents were Jewish, fifteen percent Protestant, and seven percent Catholic. Of the 85 families involved Forty-five families had one child, thirty-one families had two, seven families had three, and two families had four children.

In 1961 a second longitudinal study was initiated with 95 children of working-class Puerto Rican parents. Eighty-six percent lived in low-income public housing. In addition, a small sample of children, living in an Israeli kibbutz was studied.

Two longitudinal studies were conducted with a sample of sixty-eight children born prematurely and fifty-two children with mildly retarded intellectual levels.

A special population of two hundred forty-three children with congenital rubella (1964 outbreak) was also studied.

A total of 599 plus the small kibbutz sample were evaluated behaviorally and studied, using similar methods.

12. Thomas and Chess (1977): pp. 175-179.

Through the age of 2 temperamental factors are relatively simple to distinguish from the developing cluster of motivational, psychological and social factor; but become exceedingly difficult thereafter. Consequently, this author will not used the listing of temperamental factors for Thomas after the age of one year.

13. Thomas and Chess (1977): p. viii.

14. Thomas and Chess (1977): pp. 1-2.

15. Thomas and Chess (1977): p. 38.

After following up on and evaluating every reported incident of any deviant behavior, the research indicated that "in no case did a given pattern of temperament, as such, result in behavioral disturbance." As a practical matter, deviant behavior has multiple causes within specific environments; consequently no individual temperamental trait exists or manifests itself in isolation. The upshot of all this is temperament traits, per se, are not the roots of deviancy.

16. Dreikurs, Rudolf. <u>Children: The Challenge</u>. New York: Plume Books by Penguin Books USA Inc. (1992).

17. Ilge, Ames, and Baker. <u>Child Behavior: The classic child care manual fro the Gesell Institute of Human Development</u>. New York: Harper Perennial edition (1992).

18. Ilge, Ames, and Baker (1992): pp. 15-22.

19. Ilge, Ames, and Baker (1992): pp. 26-34.

20. Recall the role that God's hand or random chance plays in the development of our individuality is omnipresent.

21. What is personality? A dictionary definition opens the door. "1. The quality or fact of being a person 2. The quality or fact of being a particular person: personal identity; individuality 3a) habitual patterns and qualities of behavior of any individual as expressed by physical and mental activities and attitudes; distinctive individual qualities b) the complex of qualities and characteristics as being distinctive to a group, nation, place, etc. 4a) the sum of such qualities seen as being capable of making, or likely to make, a favorable impression on other people...." [Neufeldt, V. and Guralnic, D., Editors. (1994): p. 1008.]

How does personality develop? Or, what is the nature of an organized sense of self? Here we'll only scratch the surface to identify four basic self-experiences that one researcher believes is necessary for adult psychological health.

"A tentative list of the experiences available to the infant, and needed to form an organized sense of a core self includes (1) *Self-agency,* in the sense of authorship of one's own actions and nonauthorship of the actions of others; having volition, having control over self-generated action (your arm moves when you want it to), and expecting consequences of one's actions (when you shut your eyes it gets dark); (2) *Self-coherence,* having a sense of being a nonfragmented, physical whole with boundaries and a locus of integrated action, both while moving (behaving) and when still; (3) *Self-affectivity,* experiencing patterned inner qualities of feelings (affects) that belong with other experiences of self; and (4) *Self-history,* having the sense of enduring, of a continuity with one's own past so that one 'goes on being' and can even change while remaining the same."..."It is only in major psychosis that we see a significant absence of any of these four self-experiences. Absence of *agency* can be manifest in catatonia, hysterical paralysis, derealization, and some paranoid states in which the authorship of action is taken over. Absence of coherence can be manifest in depersonalization, fragmentation, and psychotic experiences of merger or fusion. Absence of affectivity can be seen in the anhedonial of some schizophrenias, and absence of continuity can be seen in fugue and other disassociate states."

"A sense of core self results from the integration of these four self-experiences into a social subjective perspective. Each of these self-experiences can be seen as self-invariant. An invariant is that which does not change in the face of things that do change." [Stern, Daniel (2000): pp. 70-71.]

22. The amalgam of changing events and circumstances, personal choices and attitudes, and fortune, etc. that continue to interplay throughout life, often result in changes in our p overall personality package, but tend to keep in tact our core-self and basic temperaments. Graduation, marriage, divorce, children, retirement are the more obvious changes that can change overall personality. The aggressive, competitive, over achiever retires to fly-fishing and becomes a calm, accepting fellow content to enjoy watching life flow on by. To the outside world this fellow's personality changed dramatically, but to the inner self he is true to his basic nature. Growth and development is life long.

23. Brooks, Robert and Goldstein, Sam. <u>Raising Resilient Children</u>. Lincolnwood Chicago IL, p. 7 (2001).

24. Ilge, Ames, and Baker (1992): pp. 29-30.

25. Remember, when Thomas is looking back into his childhood at this point, he is in his mid-60s. While it is true that an adult's cognitive recollection of childhood may not be completely factual, it is all that the adult has to construct prior events, short of hypnosis and/or therapy, which are beyond the scope of this story. Ergo recall our story's second presumption stated in Part III, Paragraph 4, above: "By using all of the known information about our early childhood experience we can reconstruct a reasonably accurate portrait of our self as a child and youth." This is the process we are entering at this point in the story.

26. Ilge, Ames, and Baker (1992): pp. 34-36.

27. Feng, Gia-Fu and English, Jane. <u>Lao Tsu, Tao Te Ching</u>. New York: Vintage Books, a Division of Random House, Part Eight (1972).

28. Rosen, Hugh. <u>See What I'm Saying: What Children Tell Us Through Their Art</u>. Dubuque IL: Islewest Publishing, p. xi (1998).

29. Rosen (1998): p. 13.

30. Rosen (1998): pp. 103-104.

31. Learning gaps occurred in Thomas's first through eighth grade school experience due to a myriad of factors: Excessive illness Inattentiveness Misbehavior

Persistence Removed from class due to misbehavior Poor teaching techniques Inappropriate homework Some perceptual problems

Thomas was the male and only child, who was used to getting his way and considered himself an adult. In the 1940's children who were pushy and included themselves in adult conversations and activities were considered insolent brats and were to not to be spared the rod. Children were to be seen and not heard. Thomas was the opposite he wanted to be seen and heard.

Constant and often harsh discipline, criticism, and strong disapproval from his mother and most teachers caused him to disengage from learning activities. He would stop thinking, draw a blank, didn't know. Because social studies, health, and science depended on reading, Thomas was a "C" student at best. Science a "C"! Thomas lived science, but it was experience-based and not symbol-based (reading). Reading is an abstraction of reality, not concrete reality. All those educational constructive theory types are saying, "See! See! I told you." And now in 2003, we know you're right, but in 1945, mainstream education didn't have a clue, particularly in the parochial schools.

As a result, Thomas had learning gaps, most notably in reading (along with everything else, phonics was not taught only sight vocabulary), writing (poor spelling—an over rated subject, and labored penmanship—a developmental issue, and arithmetic (Recall Thomas had reversal problems with his 7s, 5, and 3s). He did like art and singing, but they aren't academics and don't count. Besides, those are the first subjects cut from the curriculum when money is tight or even if money isn't tight. So, considered bright, but a puzzle as to why Thomas doesn't learn, he traveled through the parochial educational system, a closed system where everyone knew who you were—the problem child is in your class, lucky you. Is there any wonder why he loved to play, play, play alone? For Thomas play was unadulterated (no adults), pure creativity, physical development, learning, and play recreates the spirit and soul—a retreat from the fierce battles of home and school. Thomas's "destructive play" was no doubt fueled by a rage, which probably resulted from criticism, slapping, lickings, and other forms of not sparing the rod.

32. Holy Bible. (Saint Jerome's Edition of the Vulgate Version 383 A.D.) 1st Corinthians, Chapter 13, Verses 4-7.

33. Rader, Melvin. The Enduring Questions: Main Problems of Philosophy. New York: Henry Holt and Company, p 473 (1958).

34. Television New Broadcast, Cable New Network LP, LLLP. An AOL-Times—Warner Company (February 14, 2003).

35. Beardsley, Tim. "A Clone in Sheep's Clothing" Scientific American (March 3, 1997).

36. Flatow, Ira "Science Friday" Public Broadcast Radio Website: www.pbs.org (April 18, 2003)

37. Flatow, Ira (May 3, 2003).

38. Lehrer, Jim. "Human Cloning Ban Passes House" News Hour Web Site: www.pbs.org (February 28, 2003).

39. Raelian Revolution: www.rael.org/english/index.html (April 20, 2003)

40. My interpretation of the Holy Scripture (Saint Jerome Edition) Matthew 18.6. is a bit more encompassing than a strict reading, but still makes the point: "If anyone should cause one of theses little ones to lose his faith in me, it would be better for that person to have a large millstone tied around his neck and be drowned in the deep sea."

41. In her book For Your Own Good: Hidden cruelty in child rearing and the roots of violence (1990), Alice Miller coins and develops the notion of "soul murder".

42. Watson, James D. and Berry, Andrew. DNA, The secret of Life. New York: Alfred A. Knoph, p. 36 (2003).

43. Thomas and Chess (1977): p. 20.

44. Thomas and Chess (1977): pp. 22-23.

45. Neufeldt, V. and Guralnic, D., Editors (1994): p. 146.

46. Nursery Rhymes—lyrics and origins! http://www.rhymes.org.uk/

The story of Humpty Dumpty Humpty Dumpty was a colloquial term used in fifteenth century England describing someone who was obese. This has given rise to various, but inaccurate, theories surrounding the identity of Humpty Dumpty. The image of Humpty Dumpty, similar to our picture on the left, was made famous by the illustration included in the 'Alice through the looking glass' novel by Lewis Carroll. However, Humpty Dumpty was not a person pilloried in the famous rhyme. Humpty Dumpty was in fact a huge canon! The canon, Humpty Dumpty, was strategically placed on the protective wall of "St Mary's Wall Church" in Colchester, England. During the English Civil War (1642–1649) the town of Colchester was fiercely fought for by the Roundheads and Cavaliers. A shot from a Parliamentary canon succeeded in damaging the wall beneath Humpty Dumpty, which caused the canon to tumble to the ground. The Royalists, or Cavaliers, 'all the King's men' attempted to raise Humpty Dumpty on to another part of the wall. However, because the canon, or Humpty Dumpty, was so heavy 'All the King's horses and all the King's men couldn't put Humpty together again!' This had a drastic consequence for the Royalists as the strategically important town of Colchester fell to the Parliamentarians after a siege lasting eleven weeks. Earliest traceable publication: 1810.

47. Chartrand, Mark. <u>National Audubon Society Field Guide to Night Sky</u>. New York: Alfred A. Knopf, Inc. p. 31 (2000).

48. Zeilik, Michael. <u>Astronomy, The Evolving Universe</u>. New York: John Wiley and Sons, 5th Edition, p. 350.

49. Allen, Richard H. <u>Star Names, Their Lore and Meaning</u>. New York: Dover Publications, Inc. pp. 284, 268.

    "Lyra is on the western edge of the Milky Way, next to Hercules, with the neck of Cygnus on the east, and contains 48 stars according to Argelander, 69 according to Heis." (p. 284).

    "Hewitt says that in Egypt it was Ma'at the Vulture-star, when it marked the pole—this was 12,000 to 11,000 B.C. (!)—And Lockyer, that it was the orientation point of some of the temples at Denderah long antecedents to them when γ Draconis and α Ursae Majoris were so used,—probably 7,000 B.C.,—one of the oldest dates claimed by him in connection with Egyptian temple worship." (p. 268).

50. Burney, Robert. "Stinking Thinking" (April 21, 2003) www.joy 2meu.com/column.htm.

51. Dr. Greenstone believes that the Hand of God does cause events to happen in our lives and that random chance is an instrument of God's creation. The

purpose of this chapter is to show how events have affected the course of Thomas's life or your and my lives. However, the author has chosen "chance" as a literary devise or convenience to discuss the influence of events in Thomas's life. For the author to discuss these events as matters of God's plan, as in Christianity, as manifestations of Tao, or in terms of some other influence, which has guided Thomas's life, he would have to know the mind of God or the way of Tao. Needless to say, for a mortal to know the mind of God is impossible. Everybody is familiar with luck and chance. Ergo, the illustration is given in terms of luck and chance.

52. The word pachinko comes from the Japanese phrase, "pachi-pachi", meaning the clicking of small objects or the crackling of fire. Pachinko games, which date back to the 1920's, were gravity operated, simple pegboards. One player would drop his steel ball from the top of the game board; and the ball would boink-boink-boink its way down on steel pins and exit the game through openings at the bottom of the peg-board. http://www.casino-info.com/gambling_tips/pachinko.html

53. Gleick, James. <u>Chaos, Making a New Science</u>. New York:

Penguin Books, p. 122 (1987).

The plume of cigarette smoke is a 16-year old example. Today, scientists are still baffled by turbulence problems, as they were sixteen years ago. (See <u>Science and Technology Review</u>. "Into the Vortex, New Insights into the Behavior of Dynamic Fluids." Lawrence Livermore National Laboratory (April 2003). <u>www.lnl.gov/str/April03</u>

/pdfs/or_03.4.pdf-688.OKB-of:3, April:12,2003:2

"STIR a cup of tea, and watch how the tea leaves swirl and drip. Imagine what it might take to predict that movement, given only the initial forces and conditions of cup, tea, spoon, and leaves. Now add milk. The more-or-less orderly motion of tea and leaves suddenly becomes incredibly more complex, as do the forces that drive the flow and eddies of the liquids. The pathway to understanding and prediction become less clear as well. Welcome to the world of fluid dynamics—the study of fluids in motion."

"Lawrence Livermore physicists Paul Miller and Andrew Cook delved into the details of fluids on the move to simulate an experiment conducted at the University of Arizona (UA) and predict interactions of two dissimilar liquids. With the help of powerful visualization tools created by Livermore computer scientist Peter Lindstrom, they revealed the inner workings of a perplexing characteristic that, under certain situations, is key to the mixing of dissimilar fluids. Termed centrifugal baroclinic instability, the phenomenon embodies the interaction of two fluids with varying pressures and densities as they spin around each other. This fluid dynamic dance occurs in a broad range of circumstances, from deep-ocean eddies to convection currents in the cores of dying stars."

54. Models of Planetary Motion: Antiquity to the Renaissance Craig McConnell, Ph.D. Department of Liberal Studies California State University, Fullerton, CA (11/30/2003) faculty.fullerton.edu/cmcconnell/Planets.html

55. Saunders, Nicholas. <u>People of the Jaguar, The Living Spirit of Ancient America</u>. London: Souvenir Press Ltd. p. 122.

56. Glick, James (1987): p. 122.

57. Lorenz, Edward N. <u>Essence of Chaos</u>. Seattle: University of Washington Press (1996) pp. 14-15, 181.

58. Lyen, Taylor S. "Perchance…" Poetry.com (2003).

59. During the early 1970's human potential movements abounded. The quote is one that Werner Erhard used in the course of his EST Training. Obviously, everyone has the capacity to modify his act on stage at all times.

"If the whole world's a stage, where can I go to get my act together?"

60. Moses, Jeffrey. <u>Oneness: Great Principles Shared by All Religions</u>. New York: Fawcett Columbine, pp. 64-65 (1989).

61. Moses, Jeffrey (1989): pp. 28-29.

62. Feng, Gia-Fu and English, Jane (1972): Part 1.

63. Feng, Gia-Fu and English, Jane (1972): Part 21.

64. Feng, Gia-Fu and English, Jane (1972): Part 66.

65. Camus, Albert. <u>The Plague</u>. New York: First Vintage International Edition, pp. 300-301 (March 1991).

66. Holy Bible. (King James Version 1611 A.D.): 1st Corinthians, Chapter 13, Verses 12-13.

67. Conrad, Joseph. <u>Heart of Darkness.</u> England:Penguine Books Ltd., p. 88 (1995).

68. Conrad, Joseph (1995): p. 91.

69. Conrad, Joseph (1995): p. 92.

70. The symbols referred to by the harlequin man were the heads of natives that Kurtz had commanded to be severed and placed on the fence poles surrounding his compound.

    The reader may recall that Conrad's *Heart of Darkness* was made into a movie, *Apocalypse Now.*

71. Conrad, Joseph (1995): p. 112,115.

72. Holy Bible. (King James Version 1611 A.D.) Saint Matthew: Chapter 18, Verses 1-3.

73. Feng, Gia-Fu and English, Jane (1972): Part 55.

74. Greene, Brian. <u>The Fabric of the Cosmos, Space Time, and the Texture of Reality</u> Alfred A. Knopf (2004).

www.ingramcontent.com/pod-product-compliance
Lightning Source LLC
Chambersburg PA
CBHW061402280526
45784CB00001B/341